Kamloops British Columbia Canada Book 1 in Colour Photos, Saving Our History One Photo at a Time

Photography
by Barbara Raué
©2019

Series Name:
Cruising Canada

Book 15: Kamloops Book 1

Cover photo: 7 Seymour Street West, Page 4

© 2019 by Barbara Raue - All the photos in this book have been taken with my cameras. I own the rights to them.

Series Name: Cruising Canada
Saving Our History One Photo at a Time
in colour photos

Book 1-9: Winnipeg Manitoba
Book 10: Osoyoos, B.C.
Book 11: Vernon, Salmon Arm
Book 12: Kelowna
Book 13: Penticton
Book 14: Hope
Book 15-16: Kamloops

Table of Contents

Seymour Street West	Page 4
Lansdowne Street	Page 11
Lorne Street	Page 14
Victoria Street	Page 17
Riverside Park	Page 32
First Avenue	Page 44
Lee Road	Page 45
Columbia Street	Page 46
Fourth Avenue	Page 64

Kamloops is a city in south central British Columbia in Canada, located at the confluence of the two branches of the Thompson River near Kamloops Lake.

The first European explorer, David Stuart, arrived in 1811; he was sent out from Fort Astoria, a Pacific Fur Company post; he spent a winter there with the Secwepemc people. He and Alexander Ross established a post there in May 1812, "Fort Cumcloups".

The rival North West Company established another post, Fort Shuswap, nearby in the same year. The two operations were merged in 1813 when the North West Company officials in the region bought out the operations of the Pacific Fur Company. After the North West Company's forced merger with the Hudson's Bay Company in 1821, the post became known commonly as Thompson's River Post, or Fort Thompson, which over time became known as Fort Kamloops.

After the fur trade arrived in 1812, Kamloops became the crossroads for horse-drawn pack trains. In the years that followed, Kamloops' reputation as a bristling locality for trade and commerce was greatly broadened by the gold rush of the 1850s, among other things. Following the arrival of the first permanent ranchers was the railway which came through in 1893; Kamloops continued to be the resting stop for the weary travelers. Kamloops has continued to grow since then with cattle ranching, forestry and mining.

The gold rush of the 1860s and the construction of the Canadian Pacific Railway, which reached Kamloops from the West in 1883, brought further growth.

Pulp, plywood, veneer, cement, and a copper mine are industries in Kamloops. The Royal Inland Hospital is the city's largest employer. Thompson River University serves a student body of 10,000.

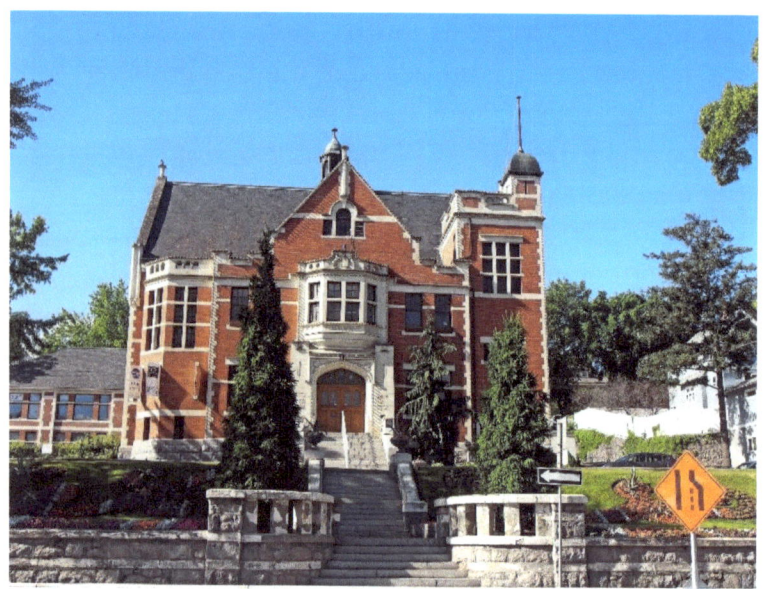

7 Seymour Street West – 1909 - Kamloops Court House – local brick and imported granite and slate three-storey building in Edwardian Baroque style – slate roof with rolled copper roof ridge, balustrades, parapeted gables, turret, cupola, oriel window, cornerstone quoins and accents, and heraldic arms

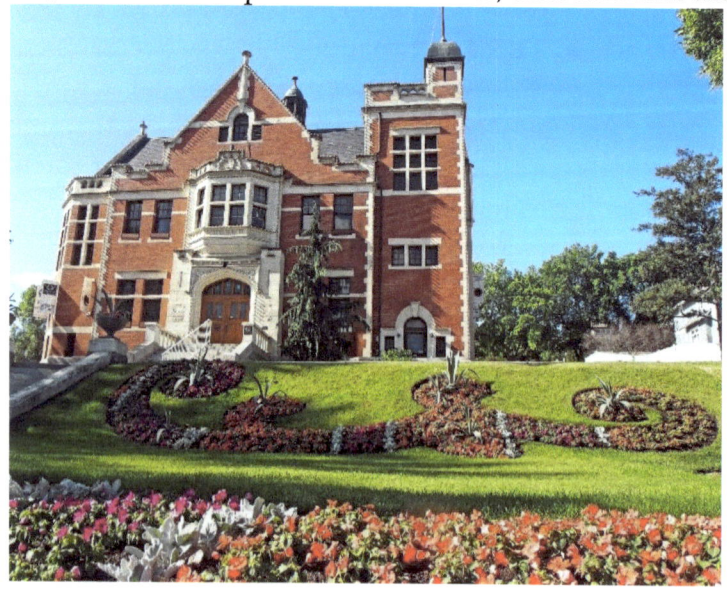

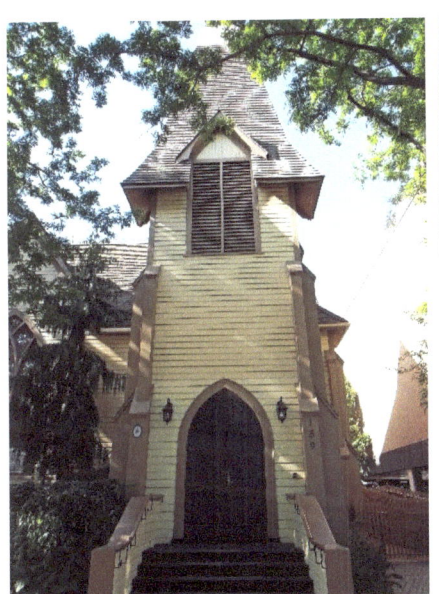 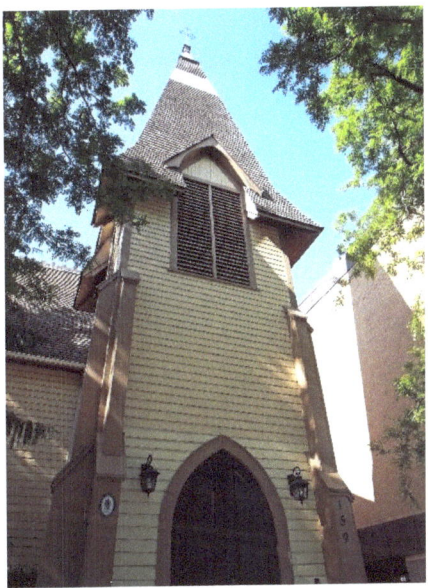

159 Seymour Street – St. Andrew's Presbyterian Church – 1887 – Reverend John Chisholm, first pastor of first Protestant Church in Kamloops, was responsible for it being built. Wood construction, Late Victorian Revival, offset square front tower with spire and gabled vents, lancet windows, corner buttress

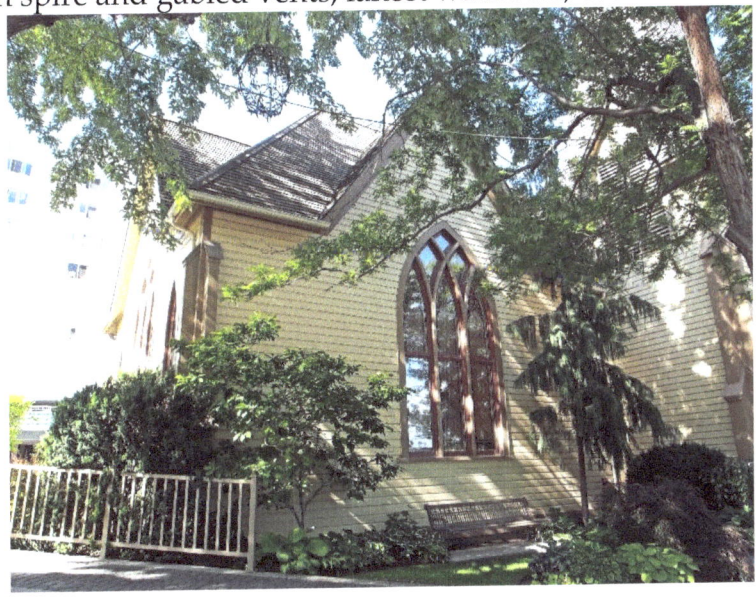

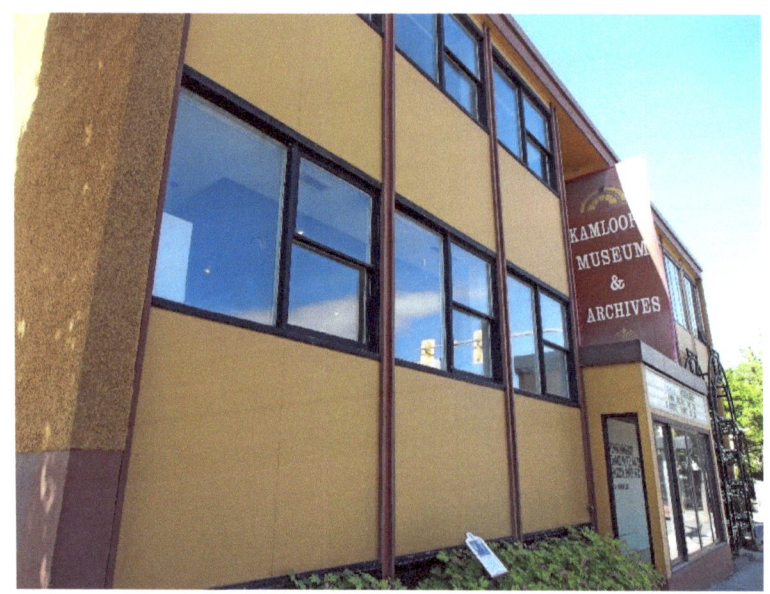

207 Seymour Street – Kamloops Museum & Archives – built in 1957

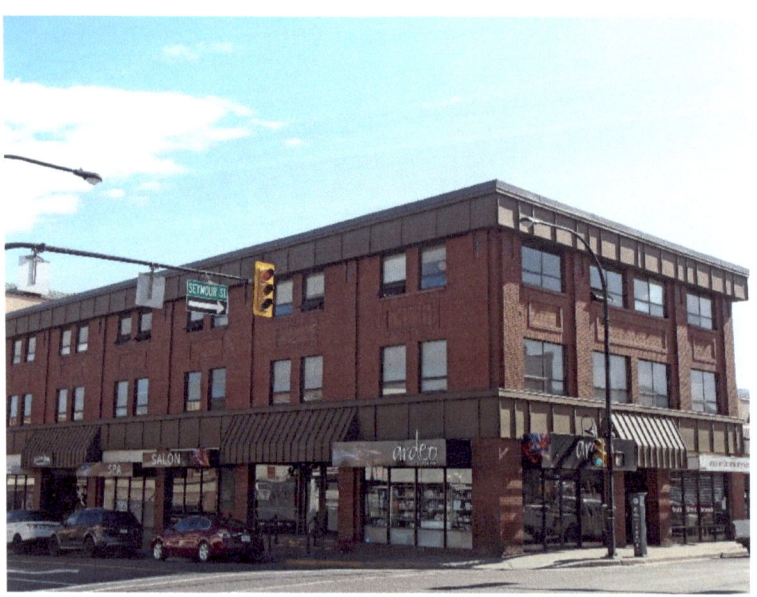

Corner of Seymour Street

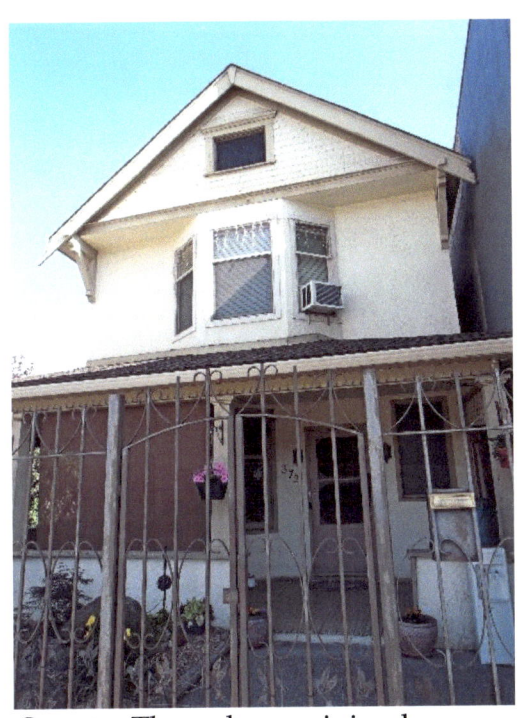

372 Seymour Street – The only surviving house on this once residential block was built in an Edwardian Builder style in 1897 by James Commacher. In 1898 it was bought by E.J. Hosker, a CPR locomotive engineer, and became his family home. Later it was bought by J.L. Gordon who owned a furniture store but also served as an undertaker. He converted the house into Gordon's Funeral Chapel and then sold it to George McPherson in 1926. McPherson's Funeral Chapel lasted until 1948 when MacLeod's Funeral Chapel took over for another 32 years. The house originally had cedar shingle and clapboard siding but plaster was added later. The dormer leaded glass windows and wrap around verandah with its square columns are original features of this house. The interior has numerous original features like fir floors, wood doors, plaster walls and a staircase with a banister.

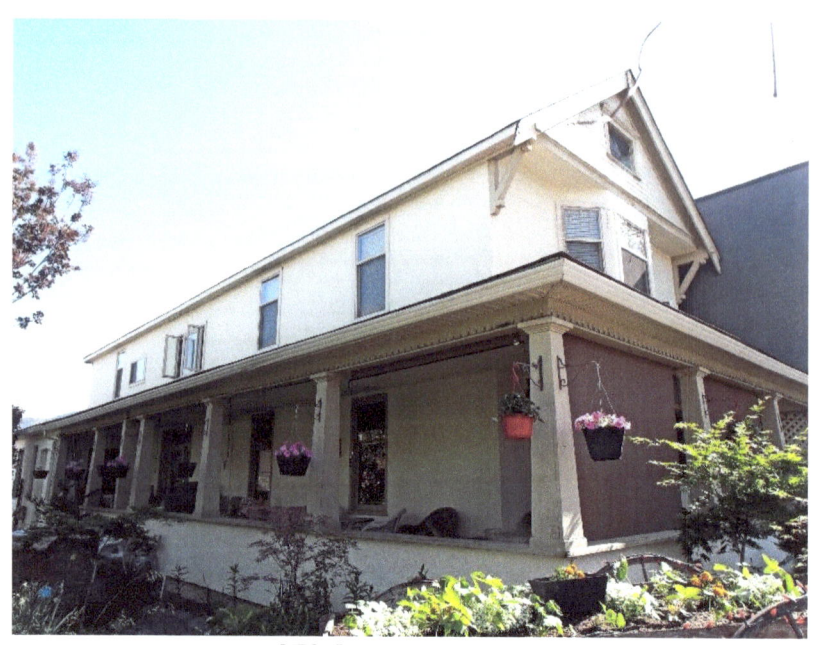

372 Seymour Street

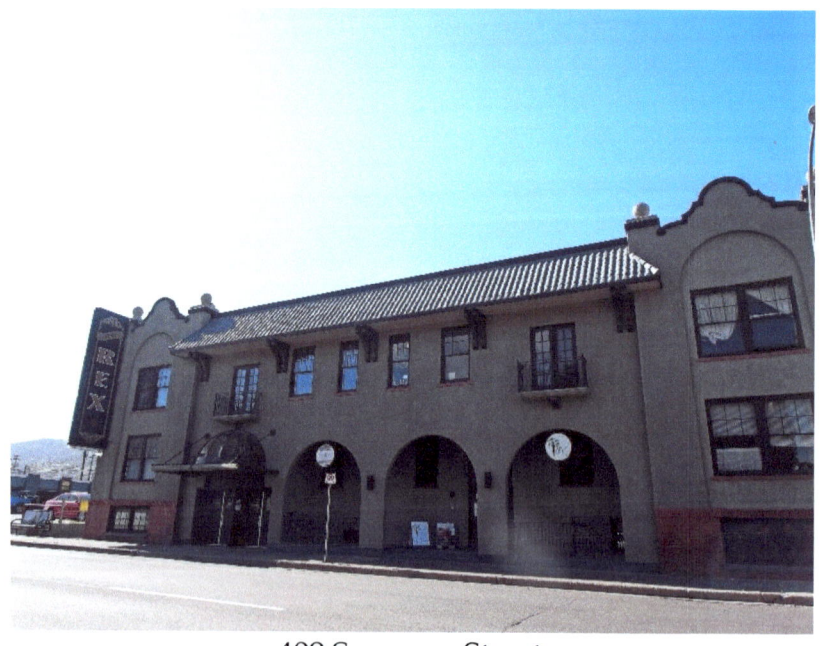

409 Seymour Street

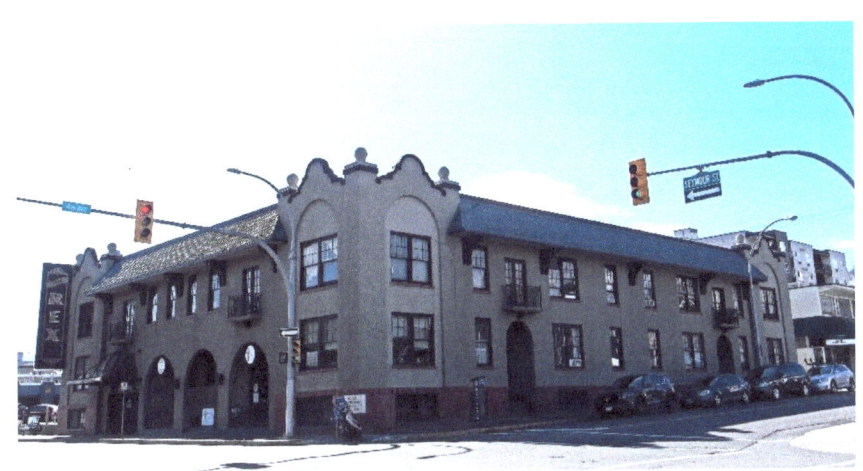

409 Seymour Street, corner of Fourth –Elk's Lodge - The Kamloops Lodge #44 of the Benevolent and Protective Order of the Elks began in 1920 with a mandate to provide community service and leadership. It contributed large sums of money to help the community by upgrading Riverside Park, sponsoring music groups, and assisting the sick and elderly. It also focused on organizing social activities like dances, concerts, and vaudeville acts.

To accommodate all its activities the Elks built a new Lodge in 1927 with club quarters, billiard room, lounge, banquet hall, auditorium and seven residential suites on the top floor. It was the first building designed in the Spanish-American style of architecture and started a trend in the city.

The auditorium had the second largest stage in the province and held an audience of 1,000. It hosted travelling shows, vaudeville, concerts, musicals, and dances. It was 'the community place'. In 1930 the auditorium became the Rex Theatre and brought the first 'talkies' to Kamloops. The latest New York equipment and design made it a popular venue.

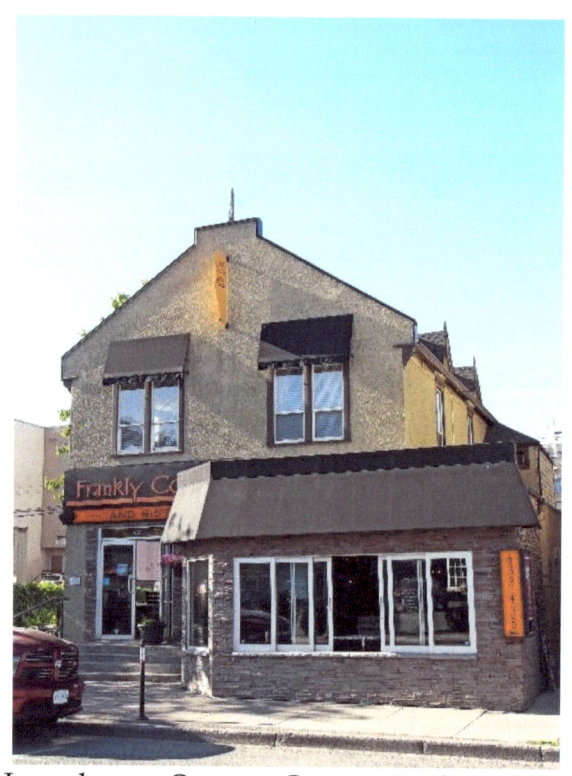

437 Lansdowne Street – Orange Lodge - The Orange Order is a Protestant fraternal organization founded in Ireland in 1796. The reference to Orange is a tribute to Dutch born Protestant William of Orange who became King of England in 1689. The Loyal Order of Orange was organized in Kamloops August 26, 1889 with nine charter members. On November 29, 1895 the Loyal Order of Orange Benevolent Ladies Association was formed and contributed to the charitable needs of the city. In 1895 this wood frame, two story structure was built as a meeting place for the organization.

The building features three gable dormers on the east and two on the west side. In 1922 renovations to the building were carried out and a covered porch was added. The Orange Order no longer exists in Kamloops.

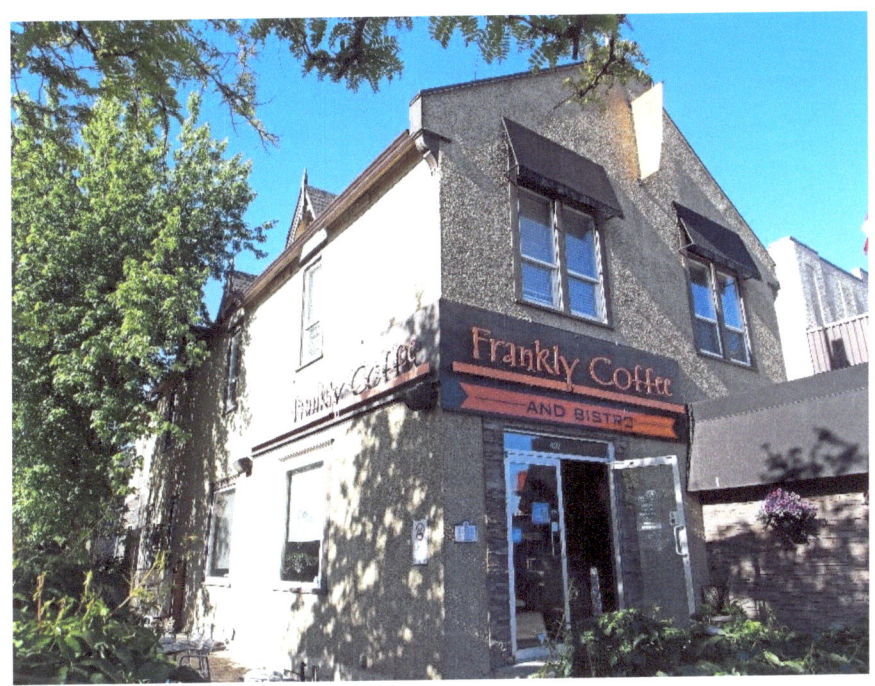

437 Lansdowne Street Street

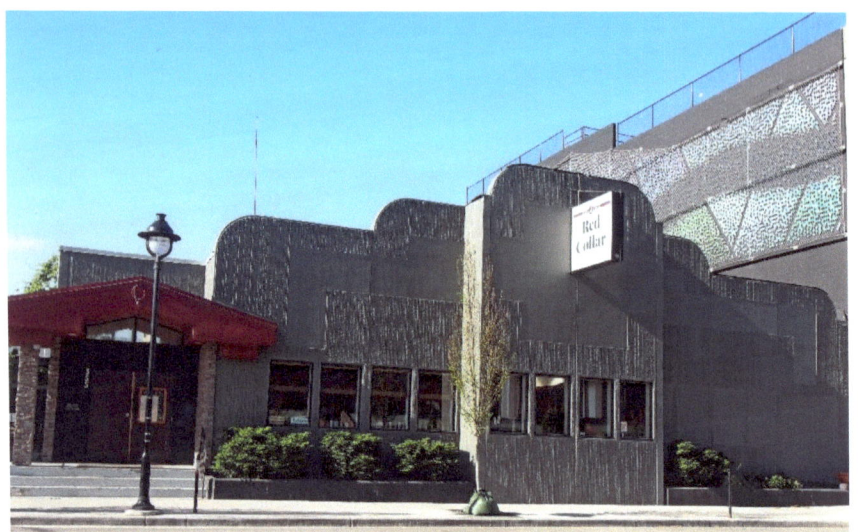
355 Lansdowne Street – Red Cellar

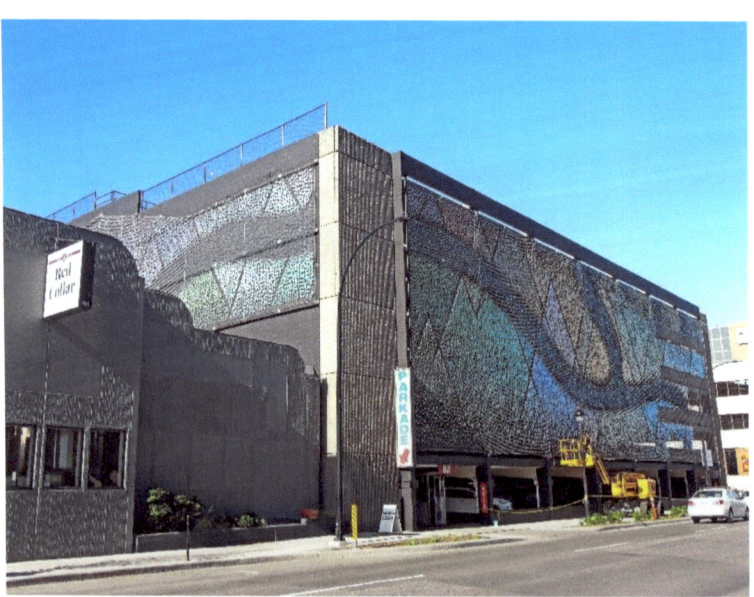
Lansdowne Street Parking Garage

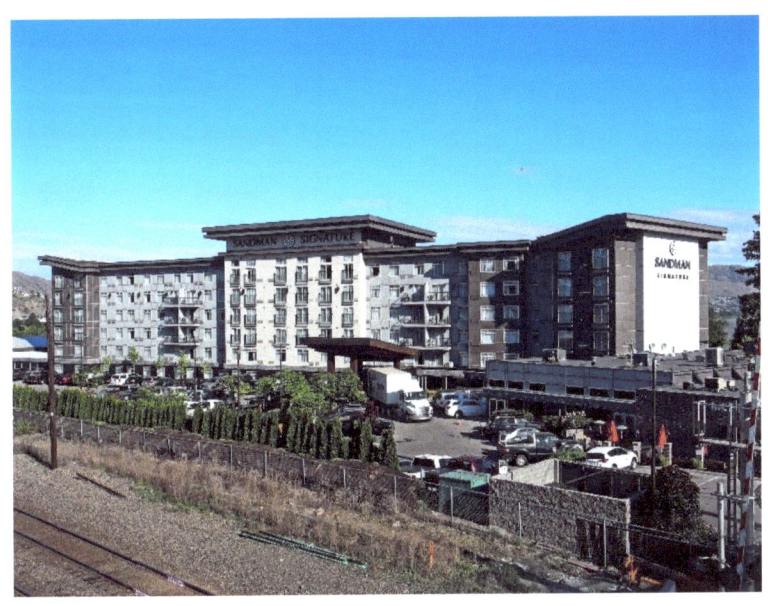

225 Lorne Street - Sandman

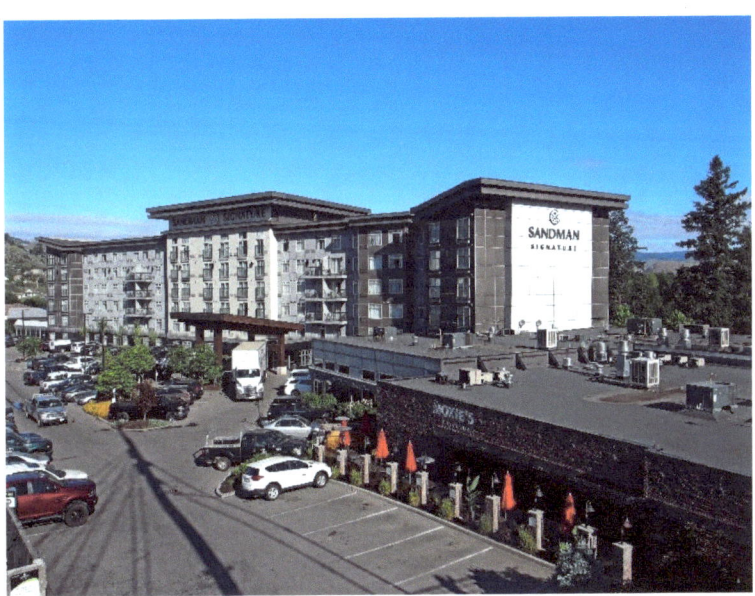

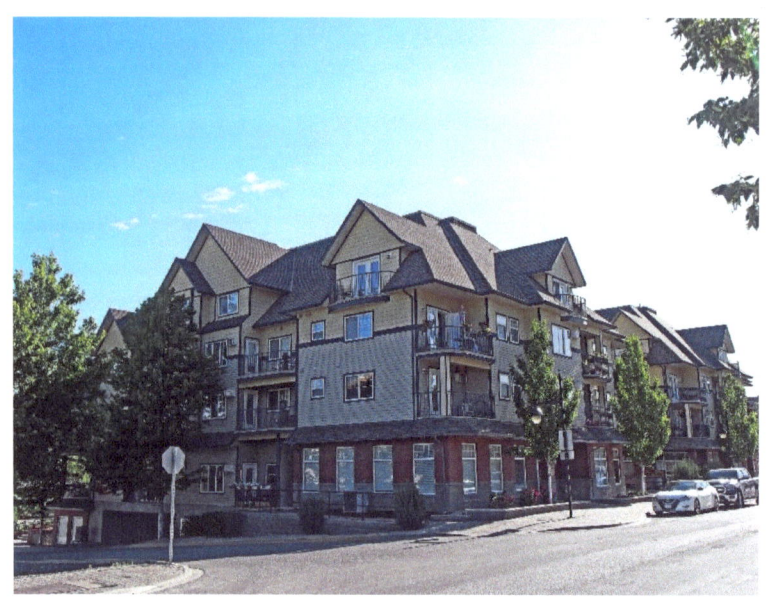
436 Lorne Street

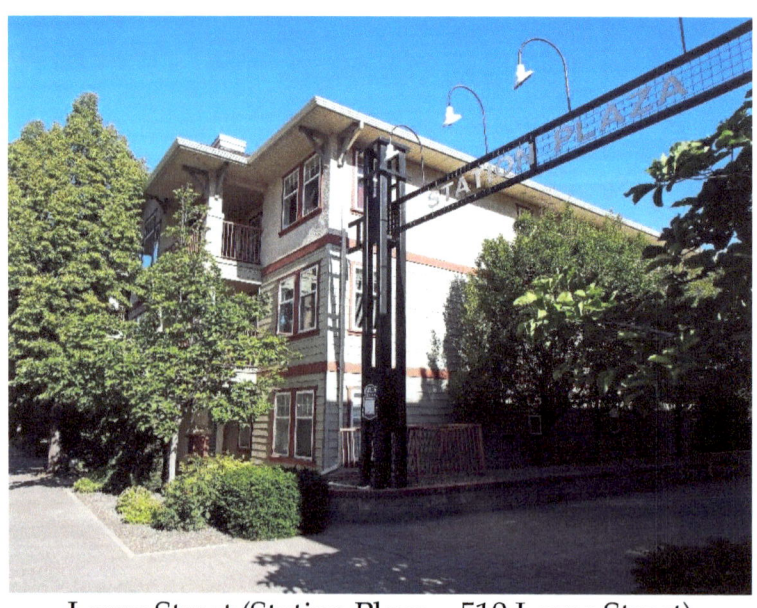
Lorne Street (Station Plaza – 510 Lorne Street)

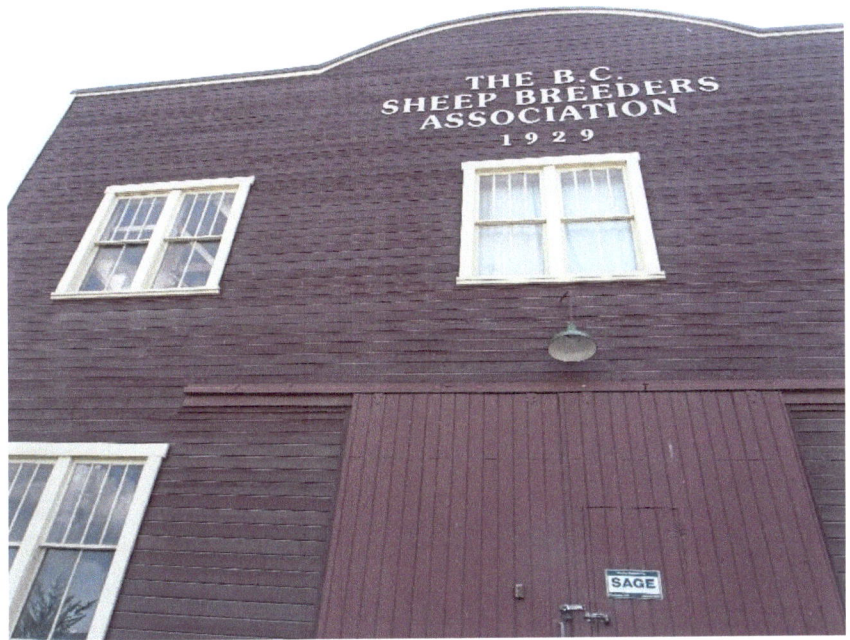

961 Lorne Street - BC Sheep Breeders' Association - The B.C Sheep Breeders Building, built in 1929, is a former industrial warehouse that serves as a testament to the sheep breeding and wool industry in Kamloops in the 1920s and into the Depression years.

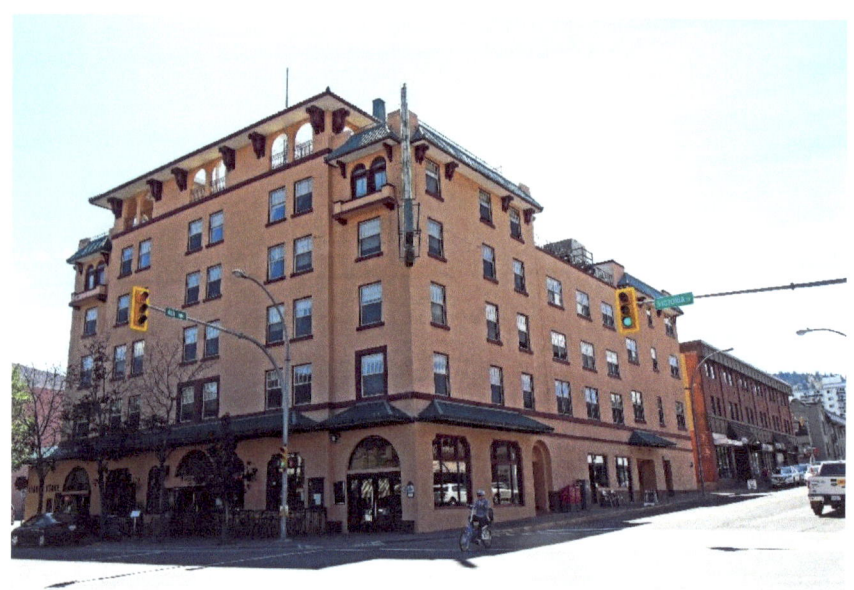

405 Victoria Street – Plaza Hotel – a five-story Spanish Colonial Revival style built 1927-1928 - metal pantile canopies, top floor outdoor roof patio with open round arches, round arches also at ground level, stucco exterior walls, large timber brackets, top floor corner balconies with French doors with semi-circular transoms; lobby with oak floors

For the official opening, there was a grand banquet and rooftop dancing. The original hotel had fifty-six hotel rooms. Additional rooms were built onto the hotel in 1948 and 1959.

The Plaza Hotel hosted a rooftop tea garden that served the Queen tea on one of her trips to Canada.

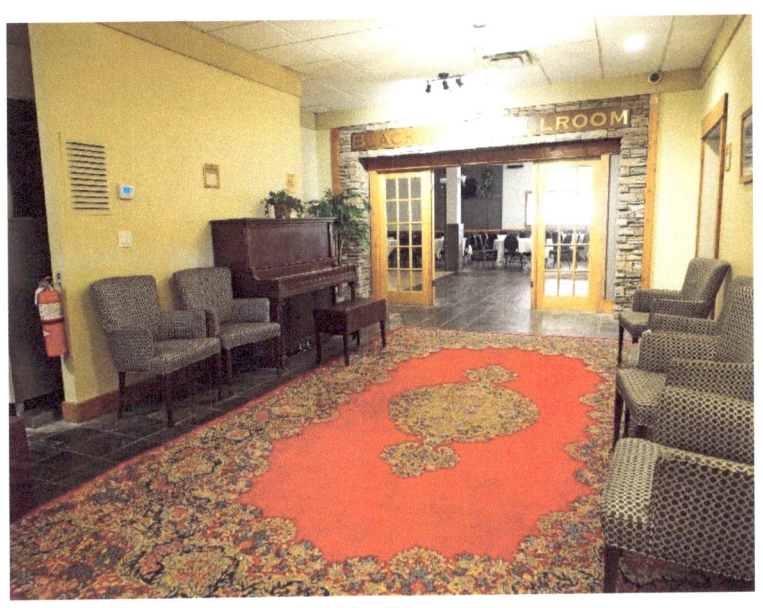

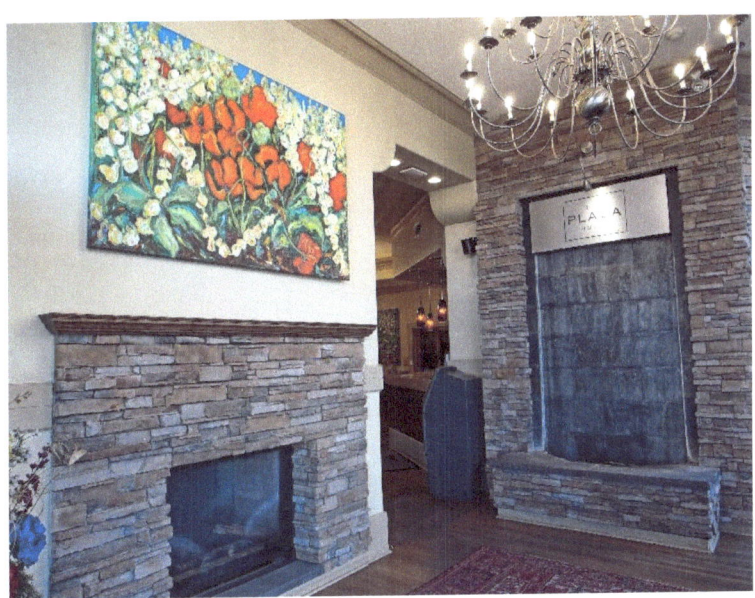

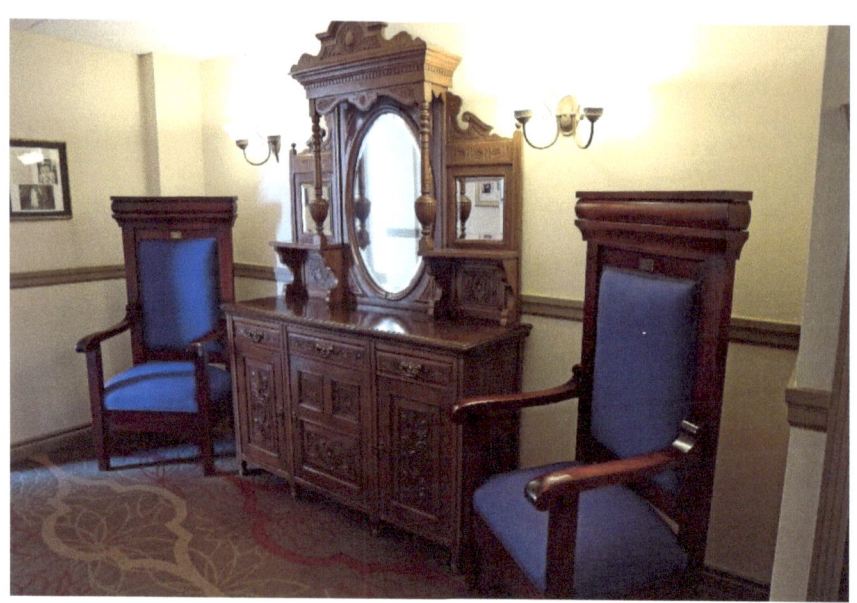

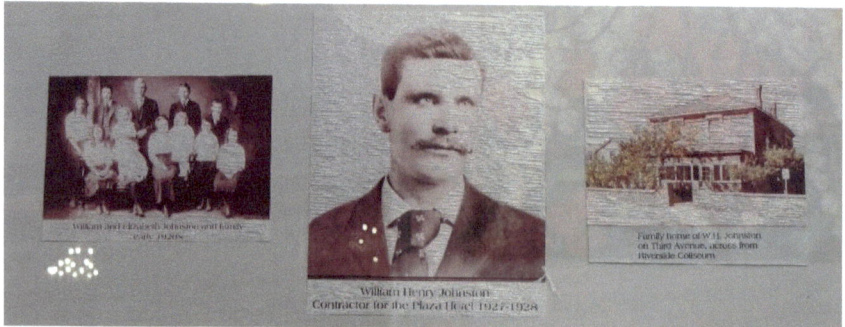

William Henry Johnson, contractor for the Plaza Hotel

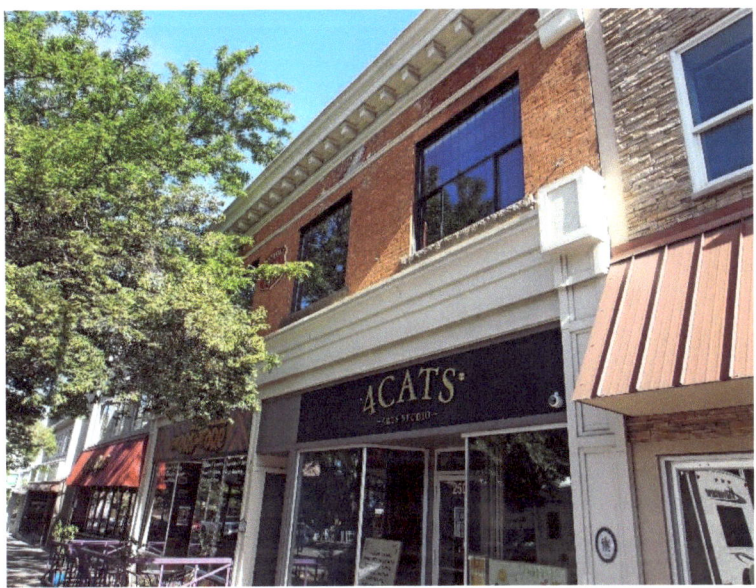

246-250 Victoria Street – The Freemont Block was built by John Freemont Smith in 1911. Smith arrived in Kamloops in 1884 and became a prospector, journalist, rancher and businessman. He was elected in 1902 as the first black alderman in Kamloops. The building features Kamloops bricks, stone window sills, scrolls on the façade, columns, a cornice at the roofline and the original Freemont Block signage.

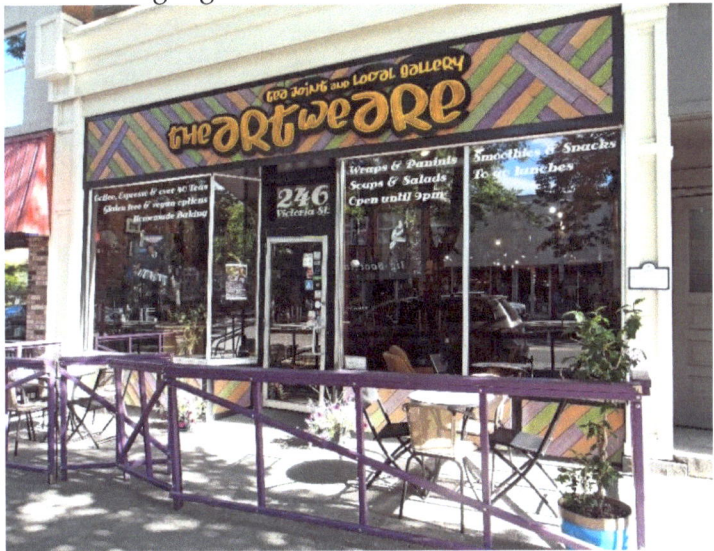

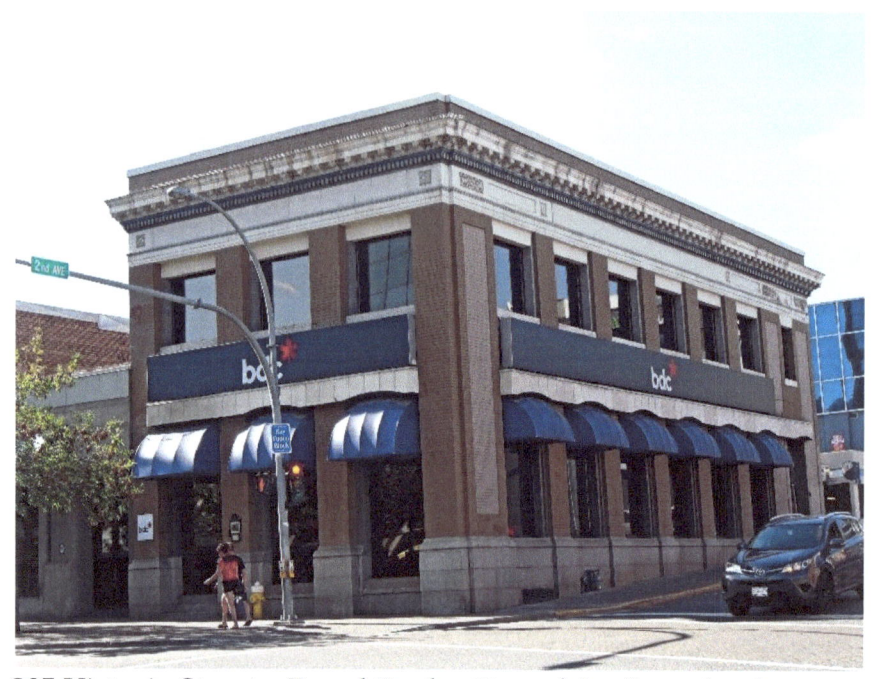

205 Victoria Street – Royal Bank - One of the finest bank buildings erected in Kamloops is this brick structure built in 1911\1912. The remains of an elaborate frieze can still be seen along the top edge of the building. The front façade once featured brick columns, arched windows, and striped awnings. The unpaved street was lined with cluster lights and tall trees.

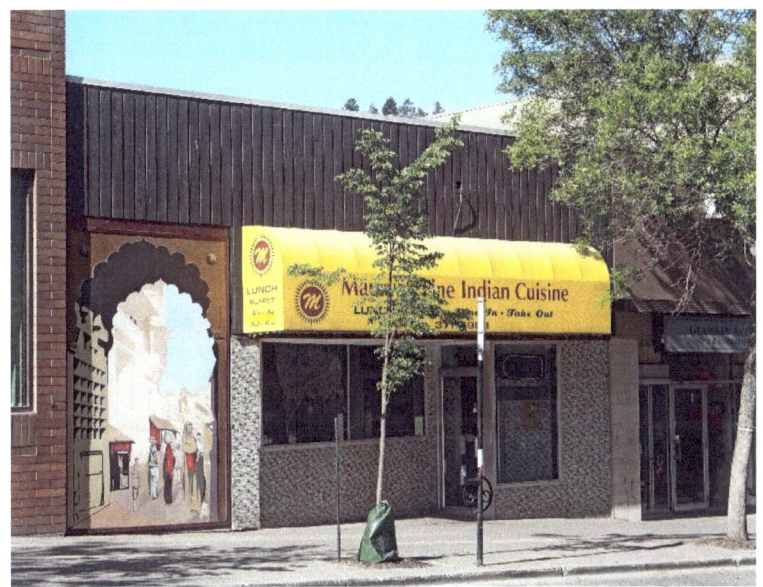

165 Victoria Street – Maurya's Fine Indian Cuisine

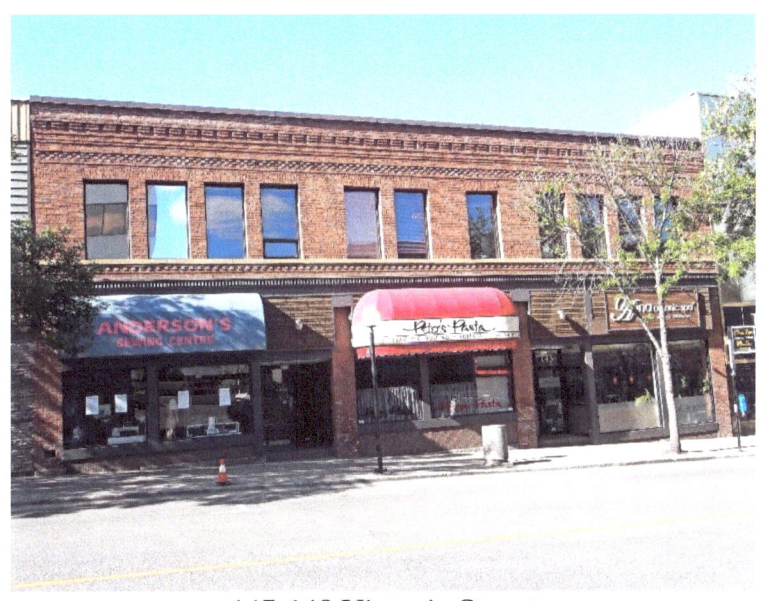

145-149 Victoria Street

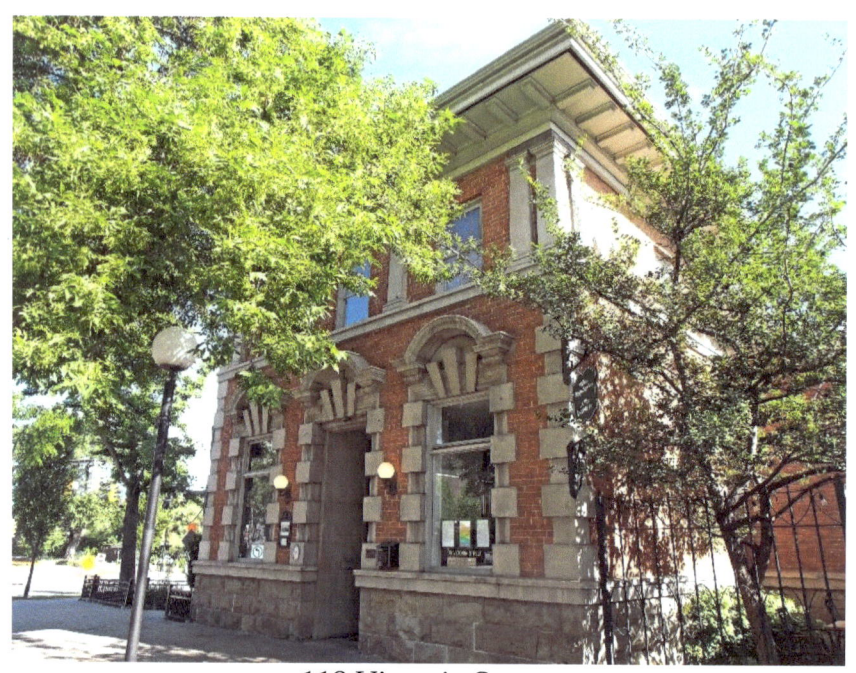

118 Victoria Street

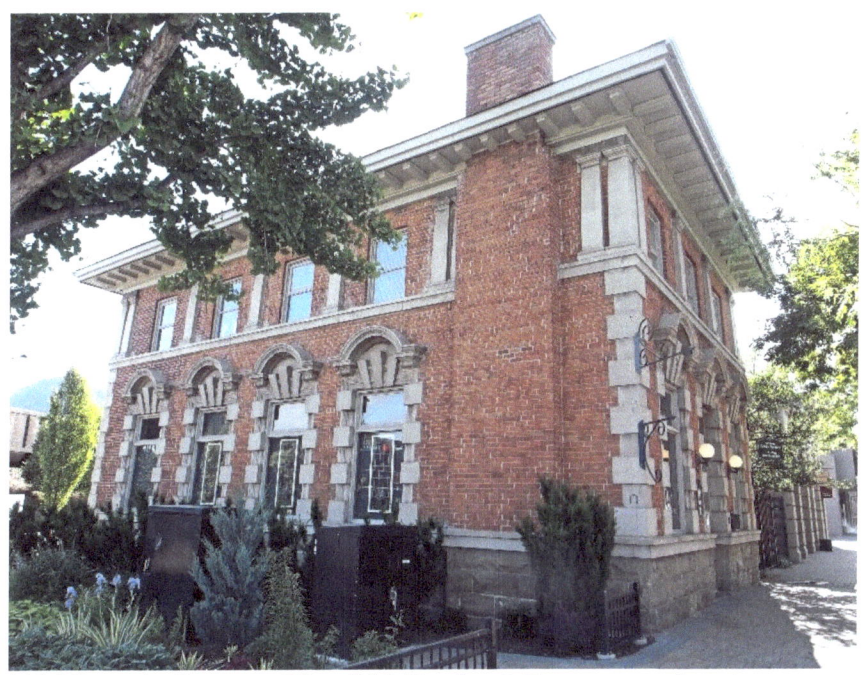

118 Victoria Street – The Old Bank of Commerce is a two-story Edwardian Baroque building with Kamloops pressed red brick and dressed stone trim built in 1904. It has a symmetrical front façade, granite foundation with raised tuckpointing, cave modillions, engaged pilasters, block quoins, external brick chimney, dentils, overscale lunettes placed over windows with giant keystones, and a hipped roof.

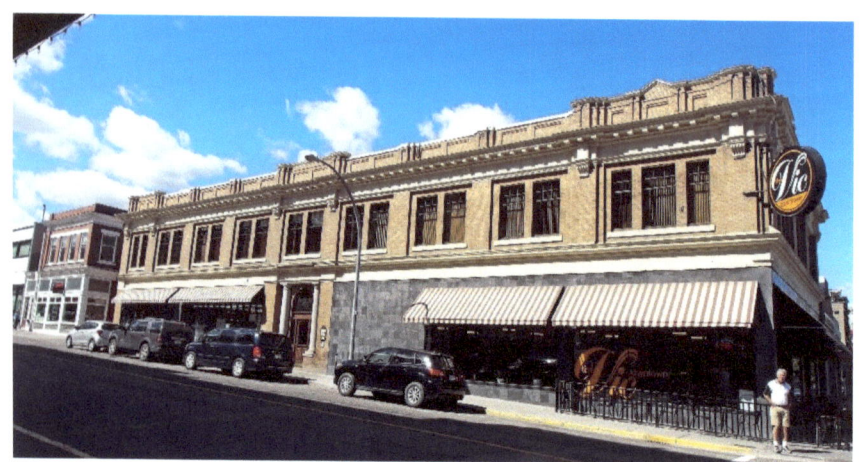

377 Victoria Street/220 4th Avenue – Ellis Block - The Godmans built this brick building in 1914. In 1917, the Galloway-Ellis Pharmacy opened on the ground floor. Partner W.O. Ellis bought the building in 1951. His drugstore remained in operation on this site under various owners until 1994.

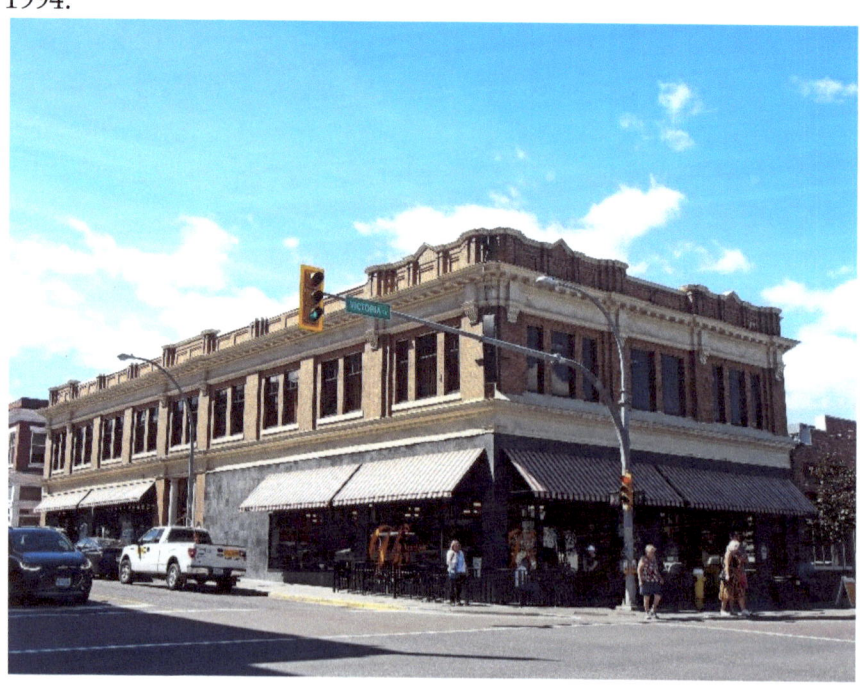

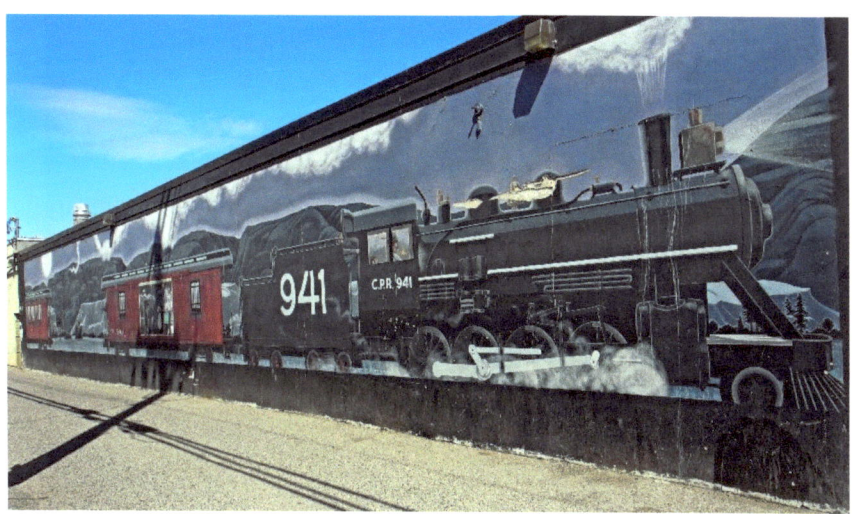

Mural by Alex Moir-Porteus with Rudy Kasmito, Joy West-Collazi, Gale Miller,

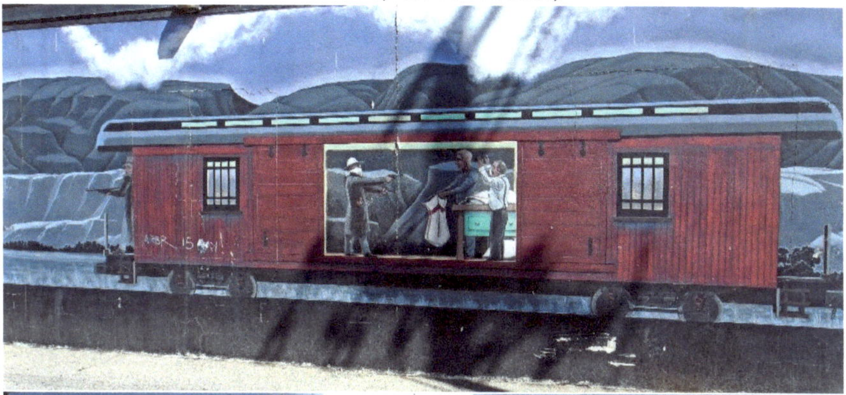

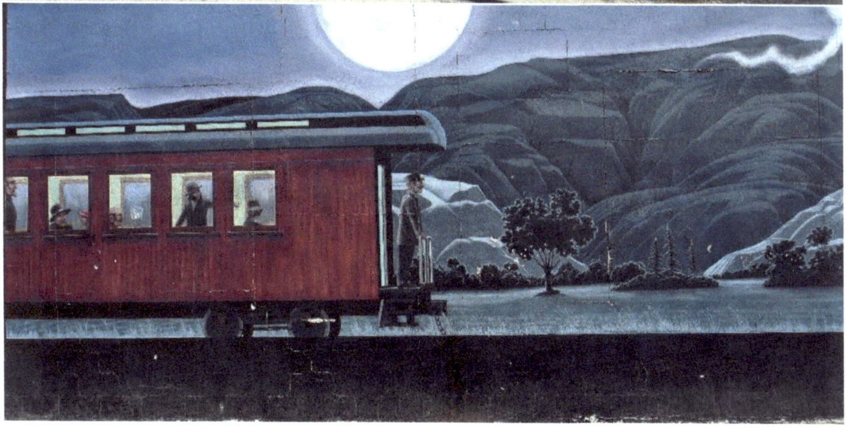

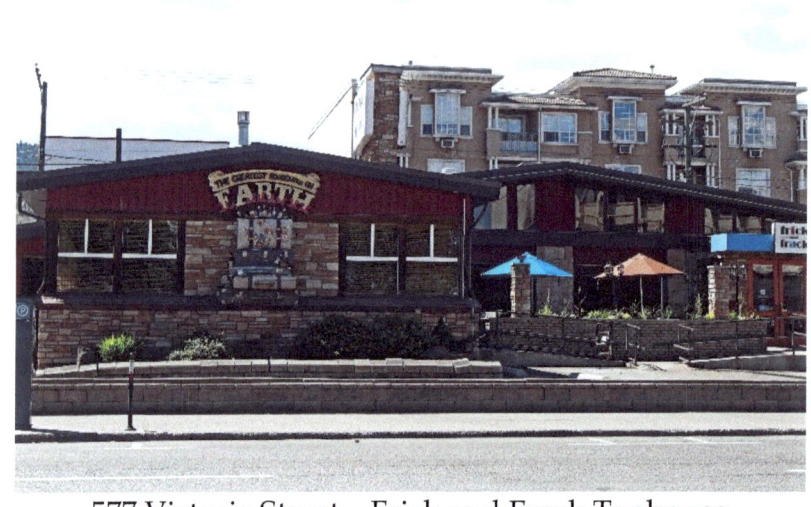

577 Victoria Street – Frick and Frack Taphouse

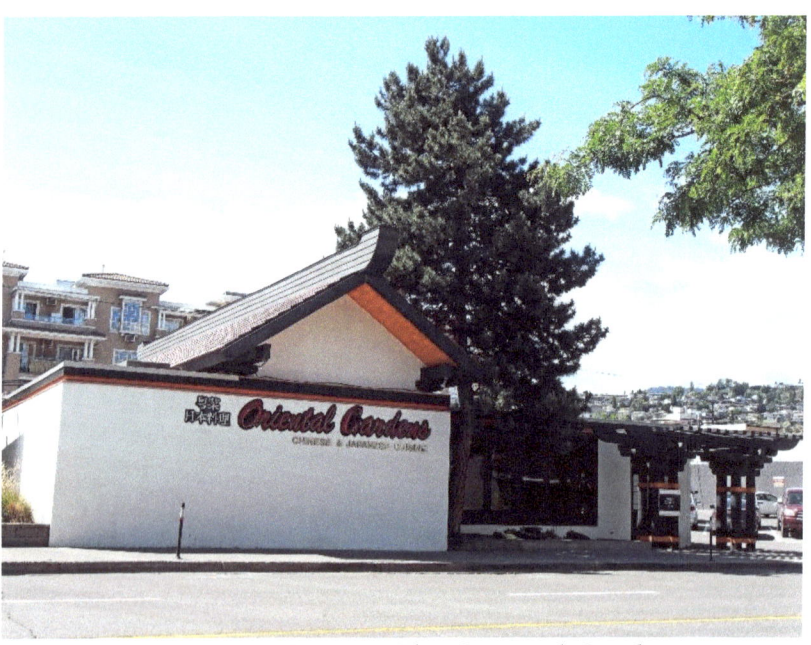

545 Victoria Street – The Oriental Gardens

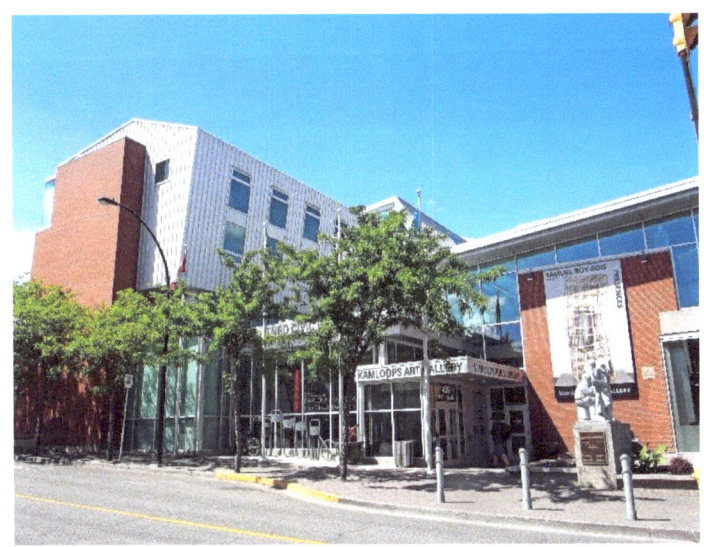
465 Victoria Street – Art Gallery and Library

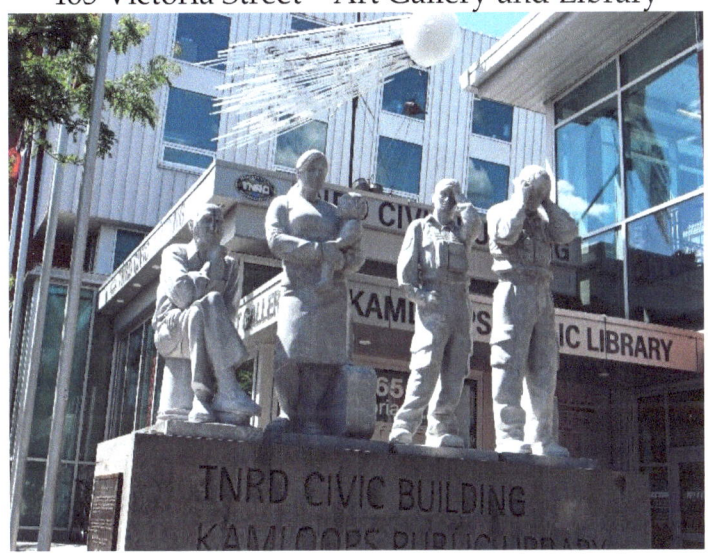
Wildfire Memorial – During the summer of 2003, the Thompson-Nicola region endured its most devastating wildfires ever. The fires destroyed 89 homes and 7 businesses, scorched 62,000 hectares of forest and range lands, left hundreds jobless and caused the evacuation of 13,000 people. Artist Cameron Kerr

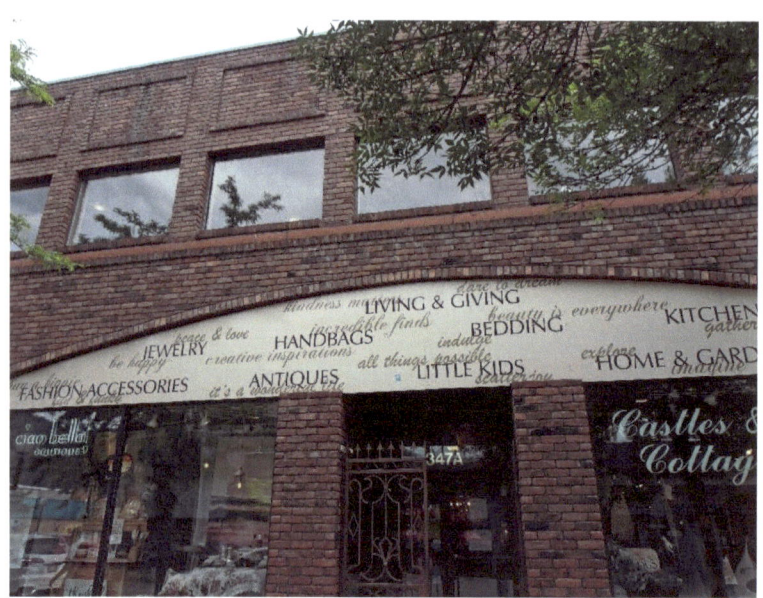

347A Victoria Street

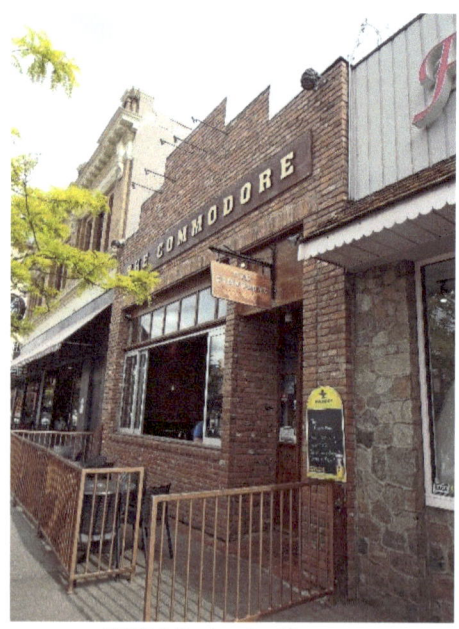

369 Victoria Street

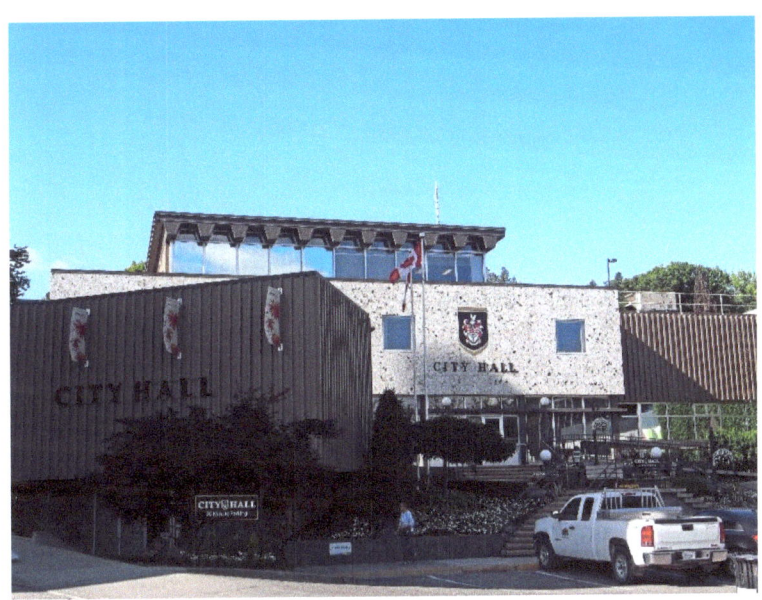

7 Victoria Street West – City Hall – built in 1963-64

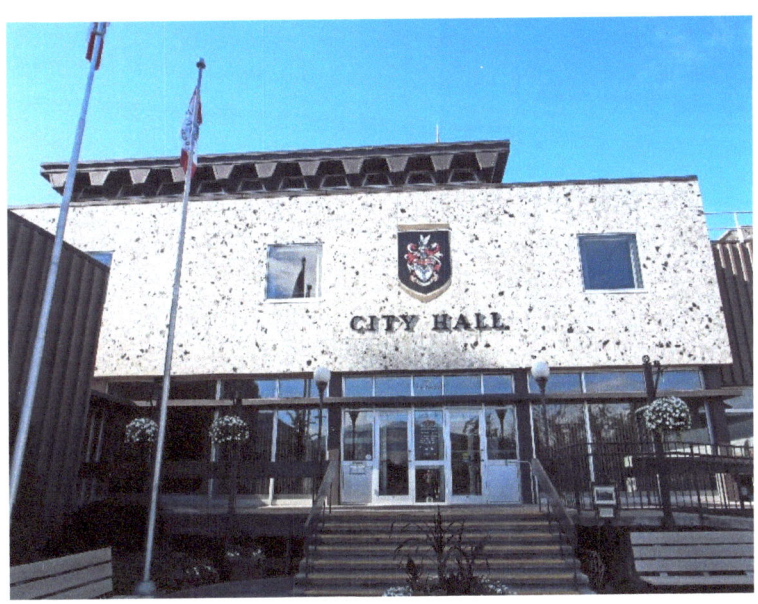

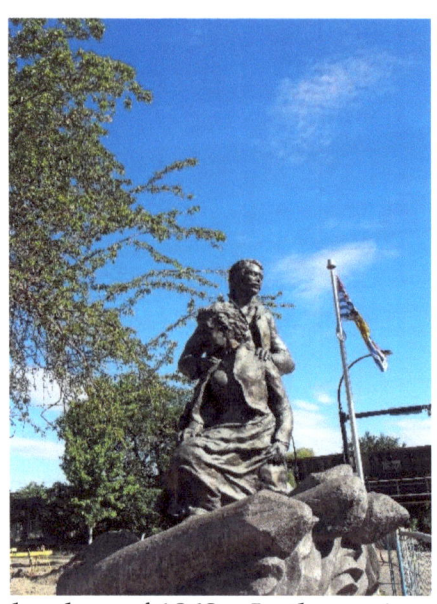

The Overlanders of 1862 – In the spring of 1862, 140 people gathered at Fort Gary (Winnipeg) to begin an overland trek across the Canadian Prairies and through the Rocky Mountains to reach the Cariboo gold fields of British Columbia. Once there, these brave pioneers helped to transform the area from wilderness to settled homeland. Food and supplies were loaded onto Red River carts for the June 1862 departure. By the end of July, the Overlanders had just reached Edmonton and their food was nearly gone. The group pressed on until they reached Tete Jaune Cache, BC, in late August. There they split up into two parties with half the group continuing down the Fraser River to Barkerville. The other half made rough-hewn log rafts and trusted their lives and their fortunes to the unknown waters of the North Thompson River. The Overlanders reached this area in October where they formed the nucleus of the new community of Kamloops. This statue depicts Augustus and Catherine Schubert and one of their children. The day after their arrival, Catherine gave birth to her fourth child. Schubert Drive is named after this Overlander family.

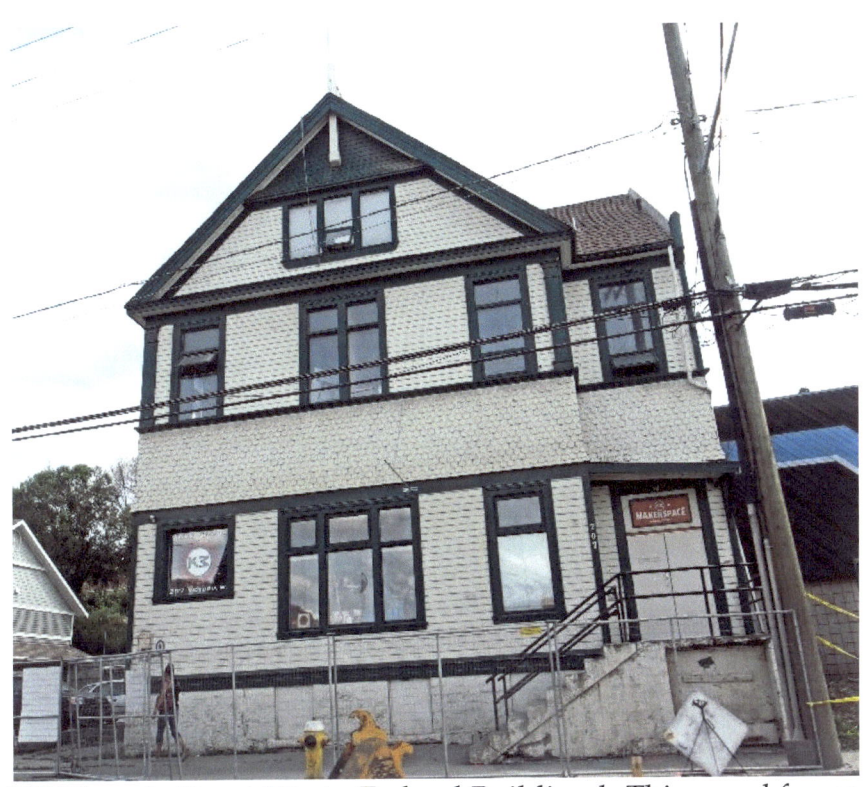

207 Victoria Street West - Federal Building l- This wood frame building was constructed in 1900 as Post Office, Lands and Titles, Customs and Indian Affairs. Architectural evidence for the early age of this building is its wood construction, cedar shingling and multi-paned windows. This is the last remaining building from Kamloops' first street.

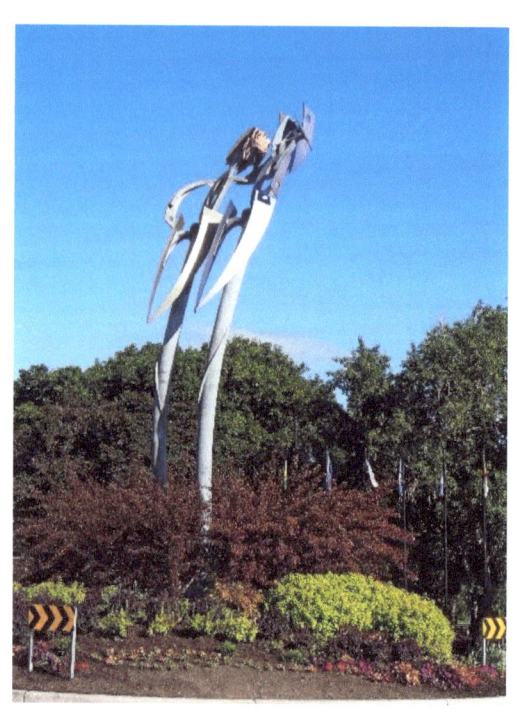

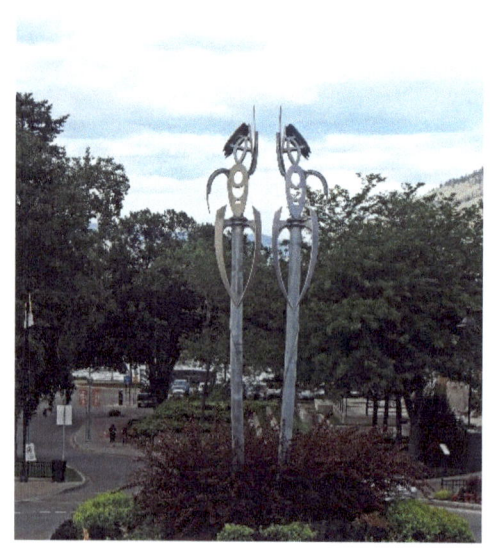

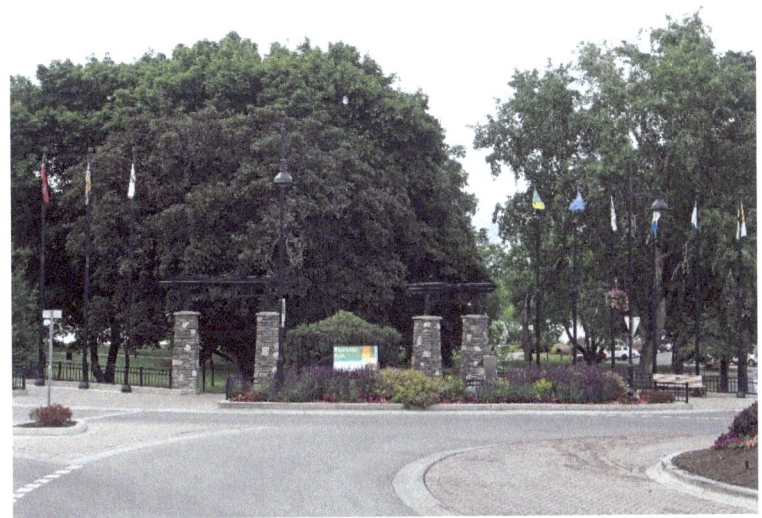

Lorne Street – Riverside Park

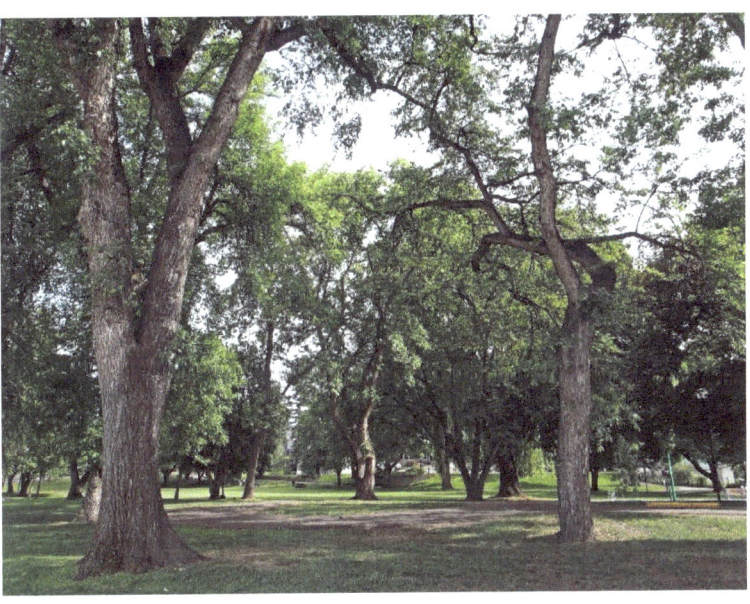

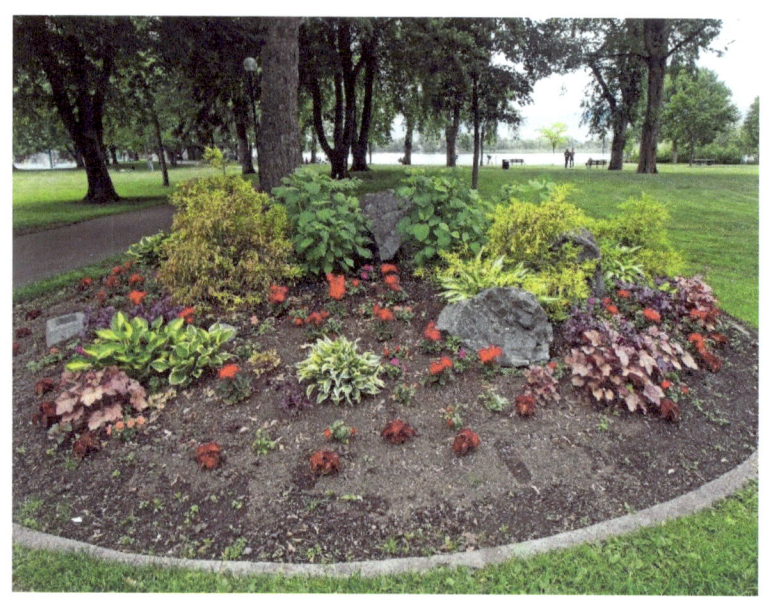

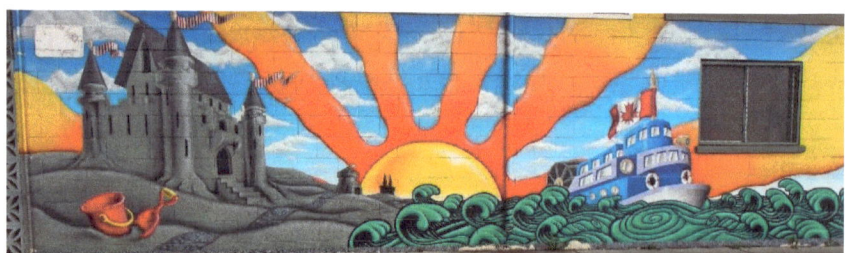
Playground mural

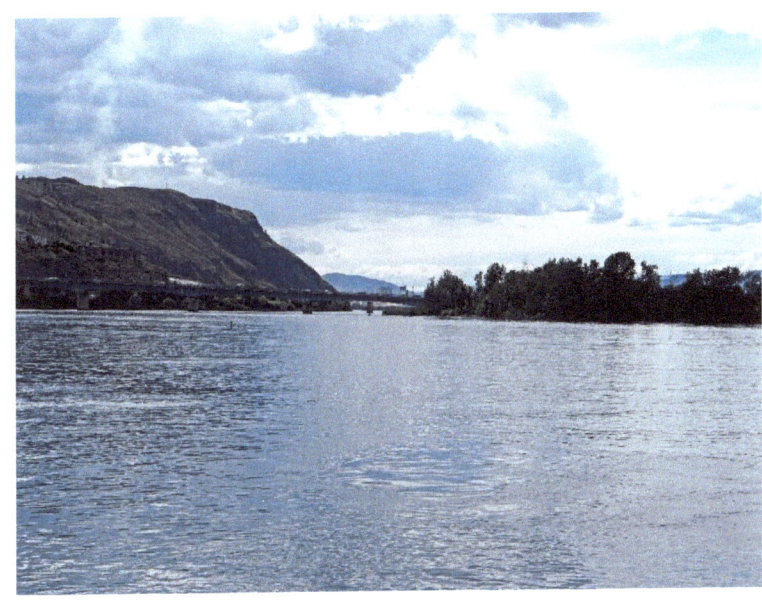

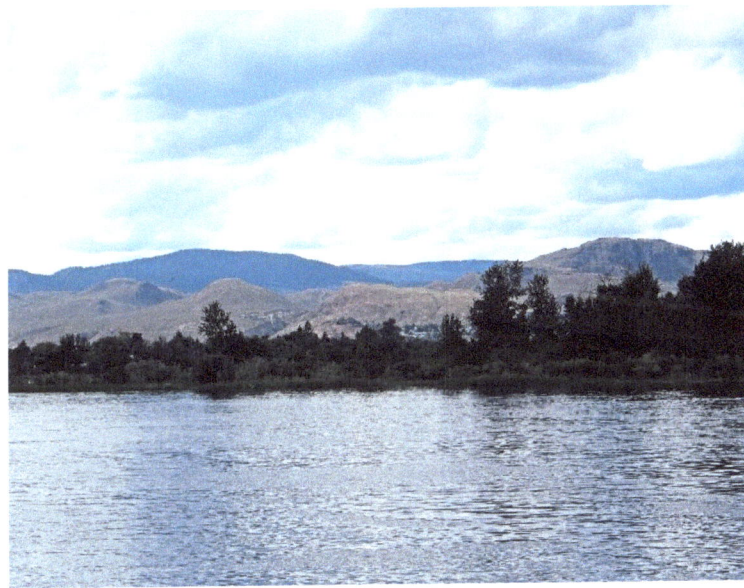

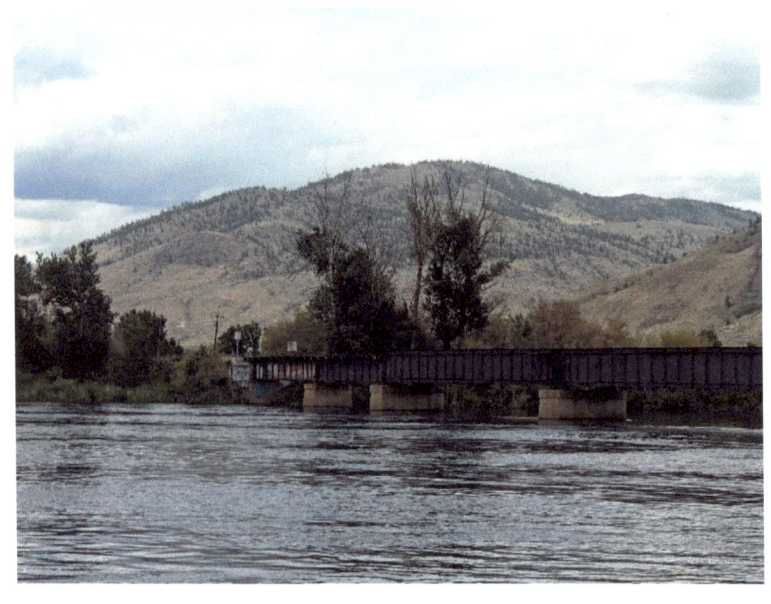

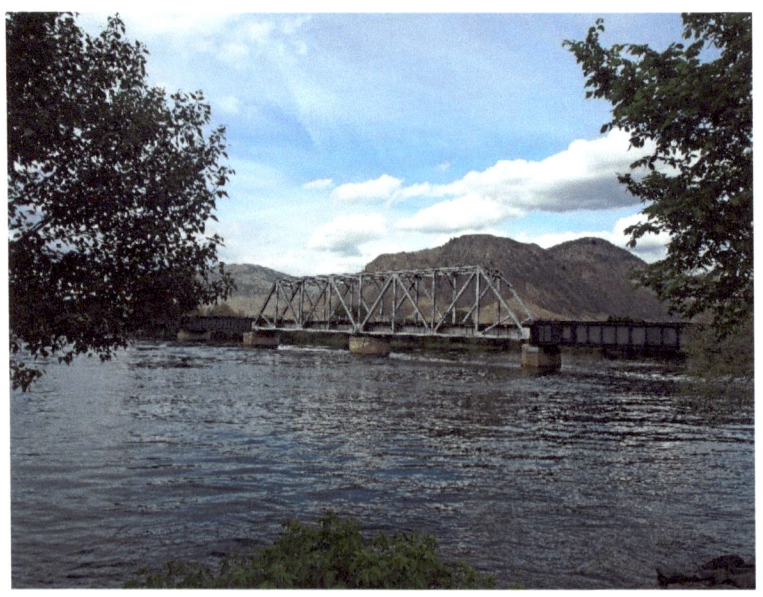

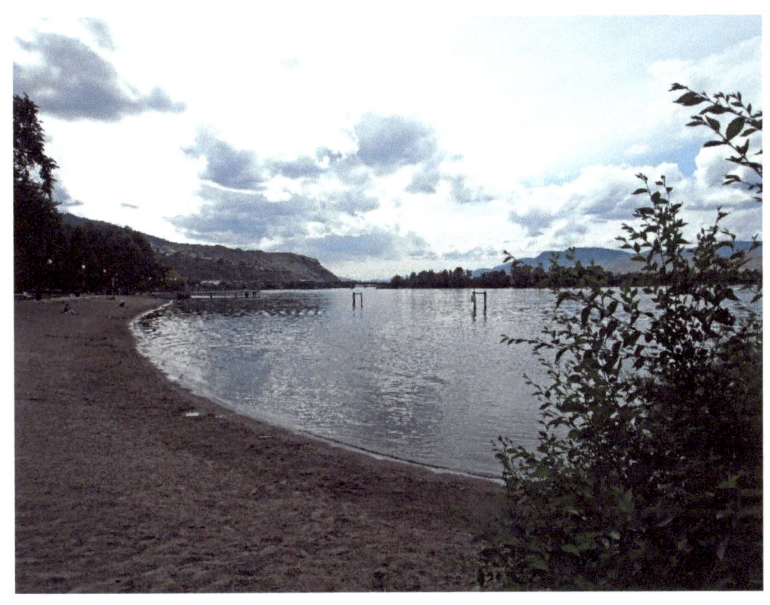

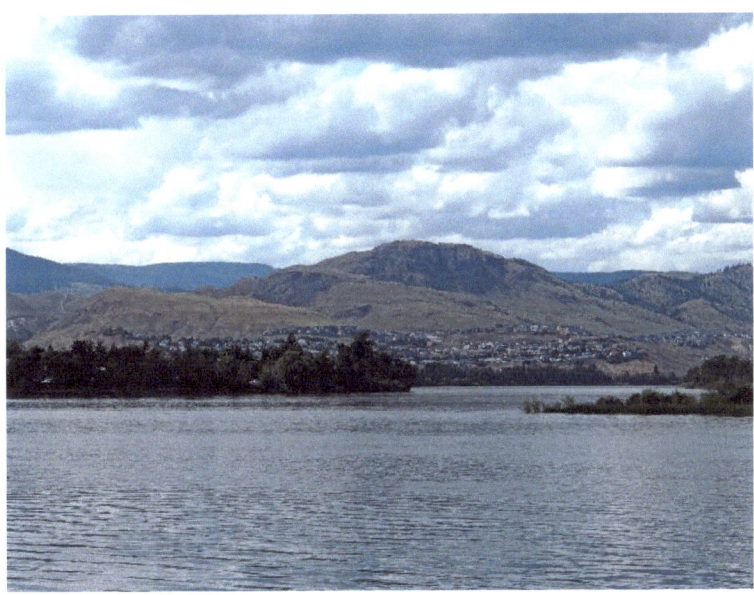

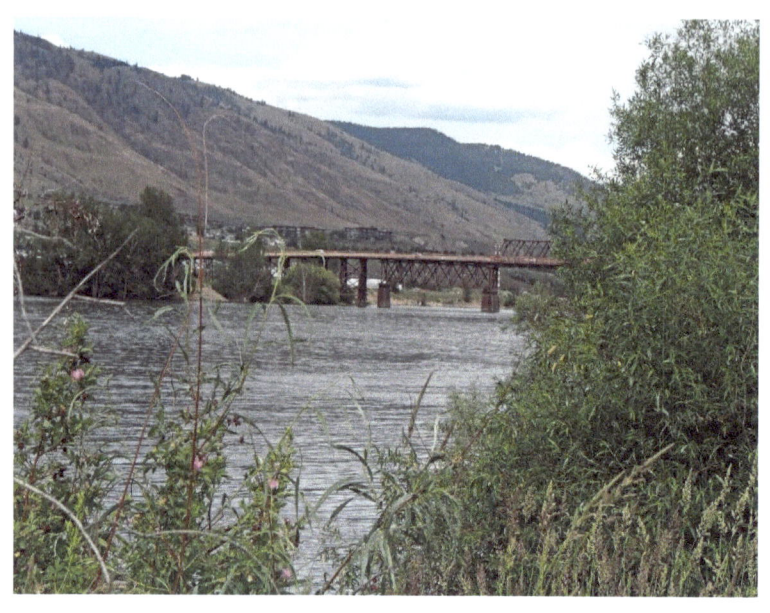

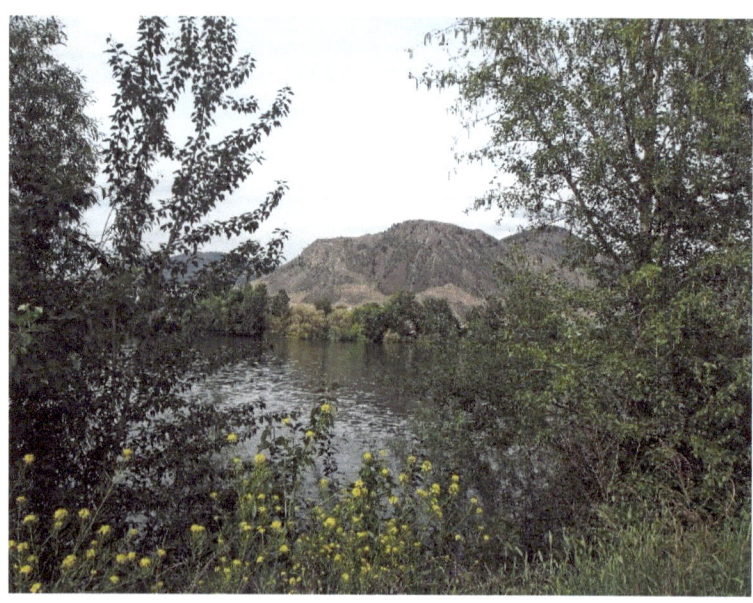

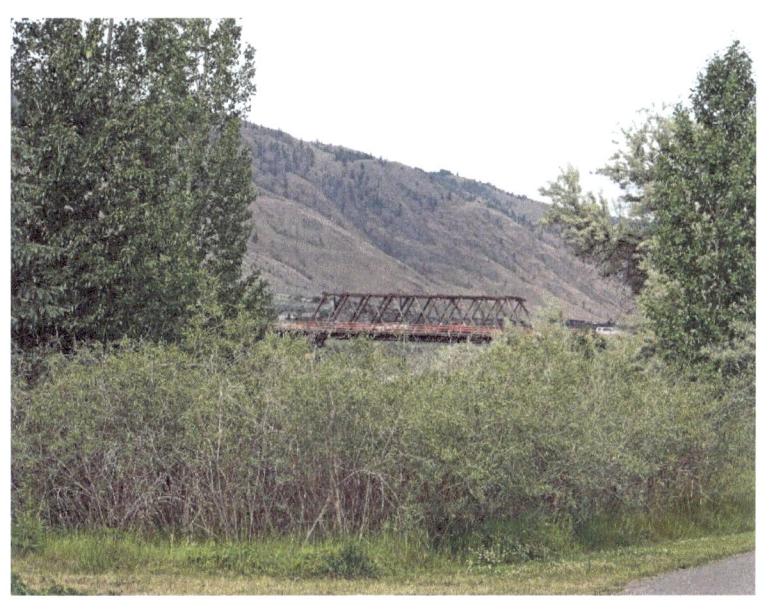

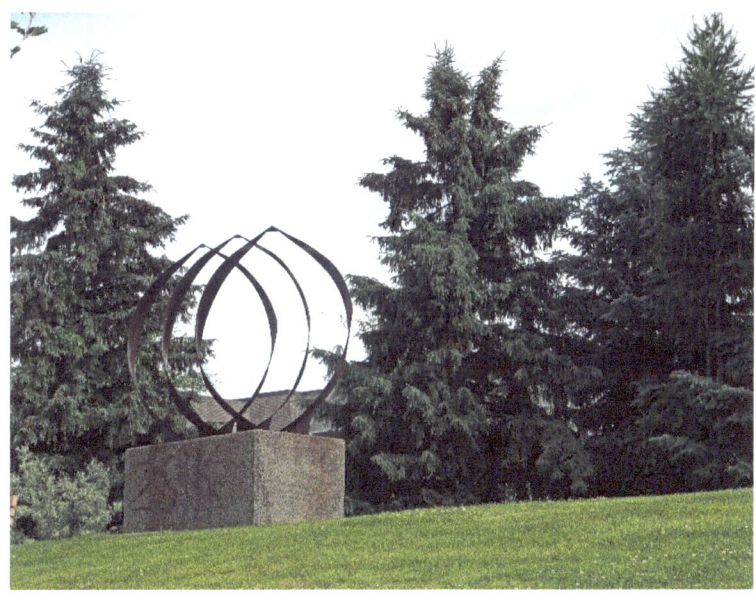

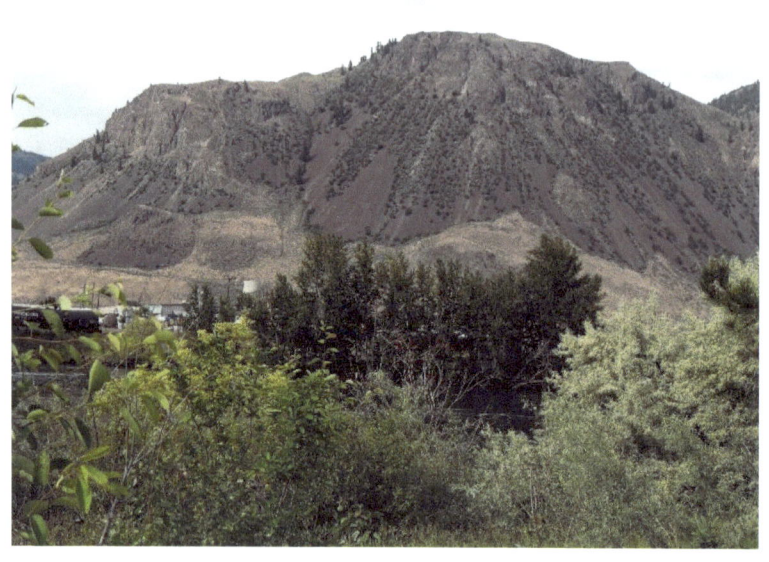

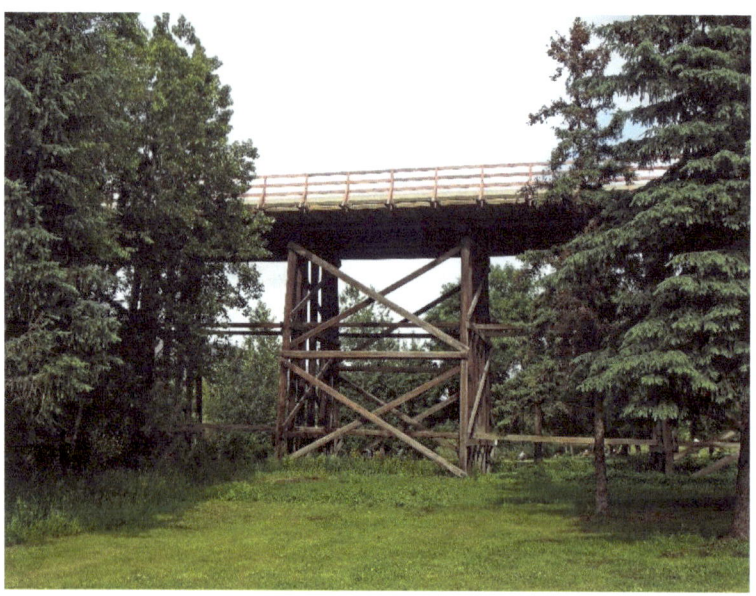

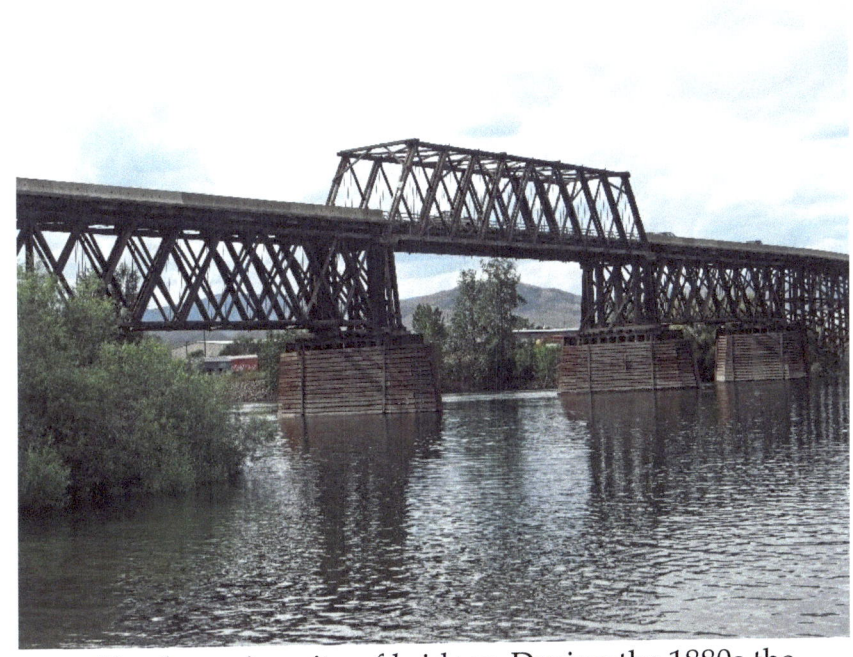

Kamloops is a city of bridges. During the 1880s the growing community of Kamloops needed a bridge to connect with its most important partner, the Kamloops Tk'emlúps Indian Band on the north shore and the predominately white population in the city. The wooden truss structure measured 300 meters and included a swing span to accommodate paddle wheelers. The official name for the bridge was Government Bridge but it has always been colloquially known as The Red Bridge.

The current bridge is the third Red Bridge and was built in 1936. The 1,200-foot (366 meters) bridge required over 300,000 feet of lumber and two pre-fabricated spans that were placed on four piers. Clearance in the center is 35 feet (11 meters) above high water and 54 feet (16 meters) above low water.

The location of the bridge is a natural crossing point on the South Thompson River before it joins the North Thompson River. For thousands of years the Tk'emlúps Indian Band of the Secwépemc Nation lived in the area as hunters and gatherers. They were nomadic during the summer relying on salmon from the river, wild game, and nature's provisions. In the winter they lived in Keekwillie pit houses along the shores of the South Thompson and Thompson rivers. Archaeological evidence of pit houses, burial sites and artifacts remain abundant to the present and can be viewed at the Secwépemc Museum and Heritage Park.

The bridge is centrally located and provides views of Mount Paul, Mount Peter and the conjunction of the South Thompson and North Thompson Rivers.

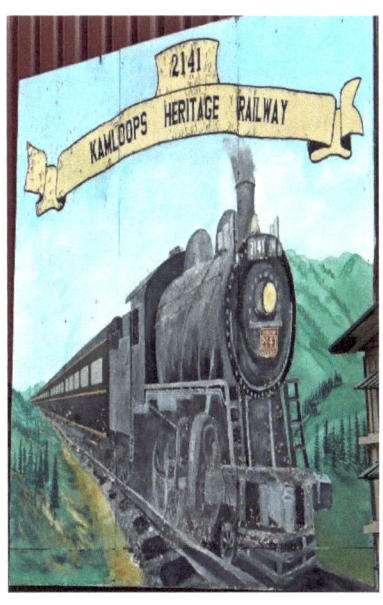

Kamloops Heritage Railway

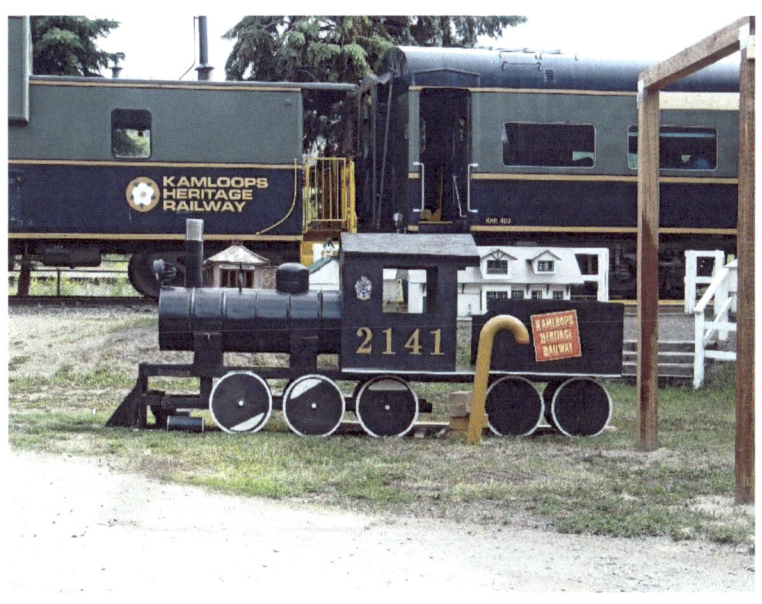

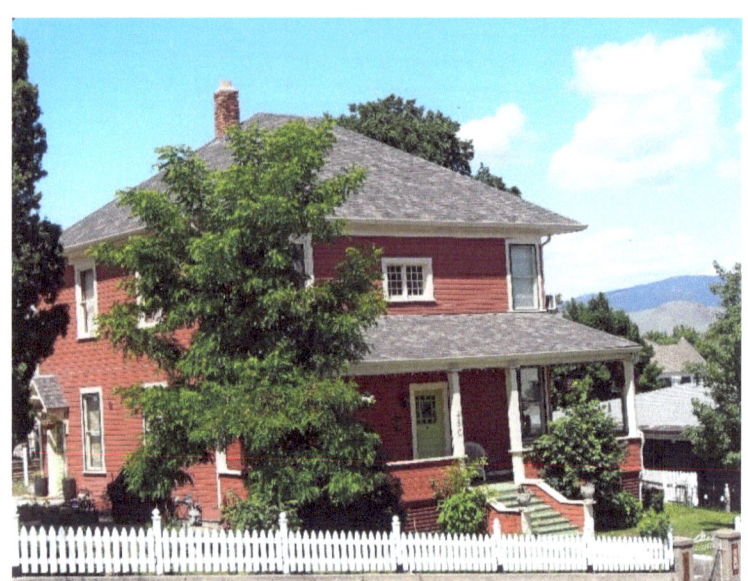

480 First Avenue

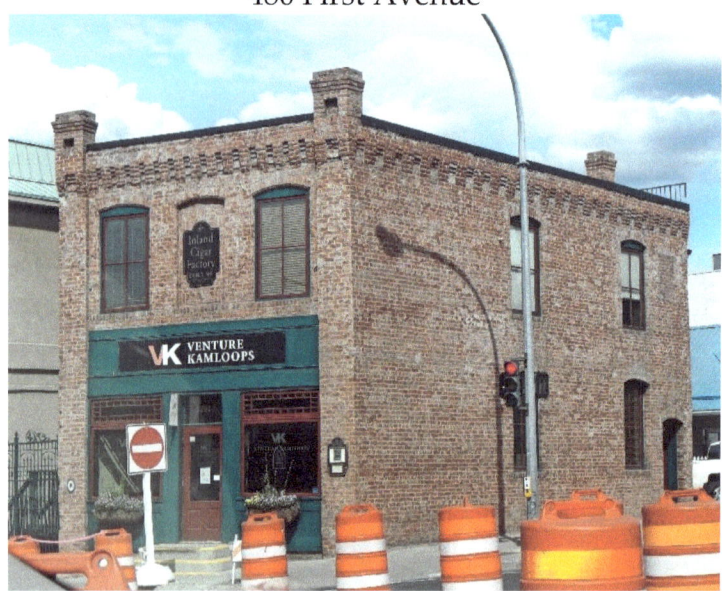

297 First Avenue – The Inland Cigar Factory is a two-story red brick Victoria era commercial building with a corbelled cornice, arched second floor window openings and a blind arched opening above central entry with rubbed brick outline and herringbone infill.

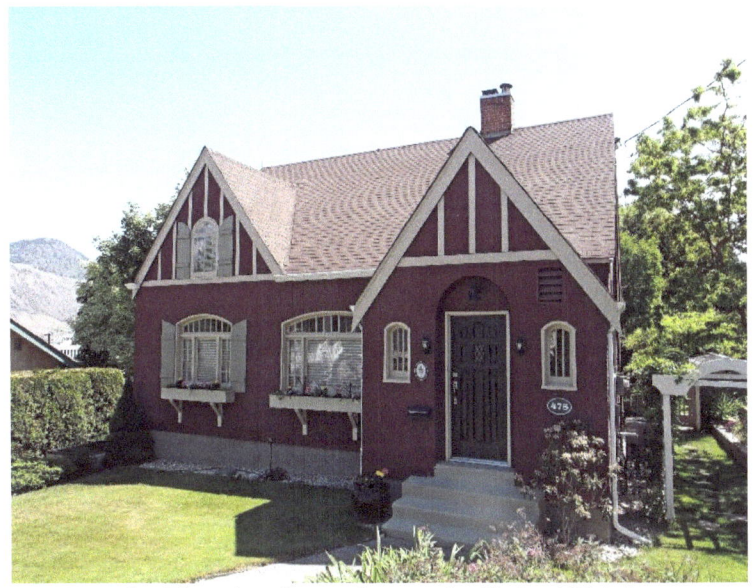

475 Lee Road - This Art Deco house built in 1931 features plaster siding, wood trim, arched windows with multi-pane glass and decorative shutters.

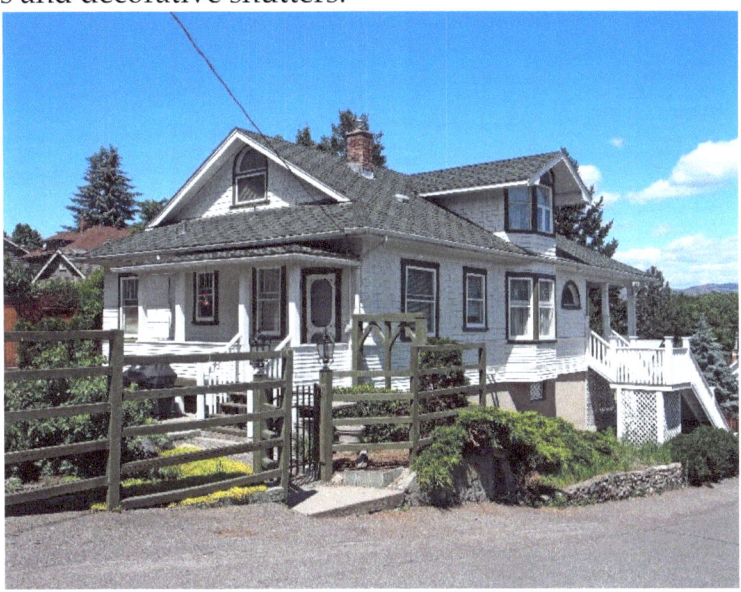

Lee Road

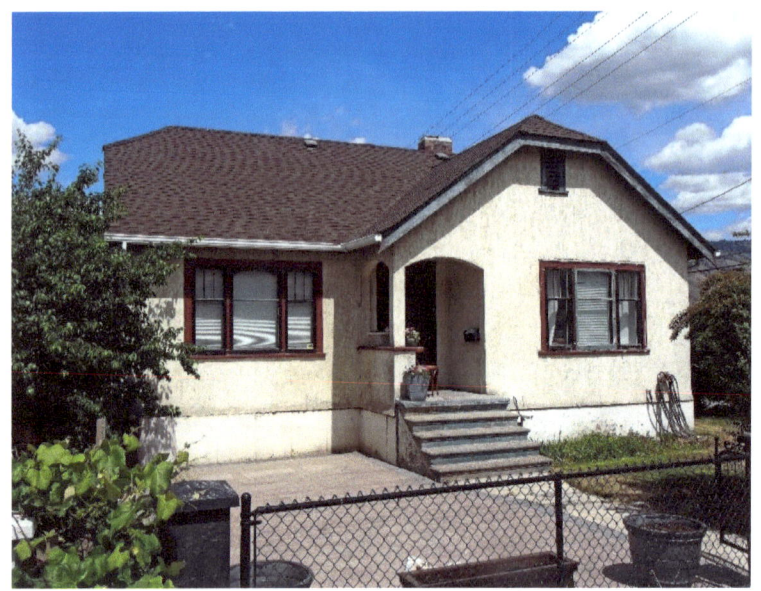
Columbia Street – chipped gable

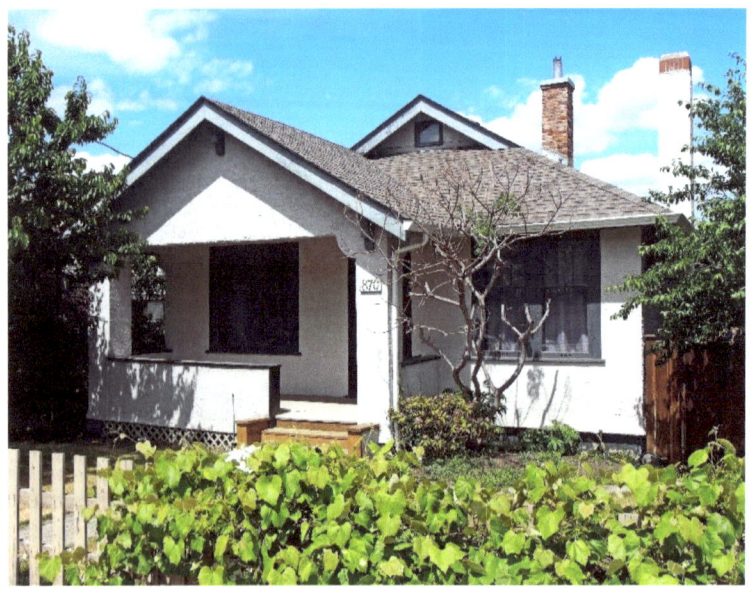
870 Columbia Street

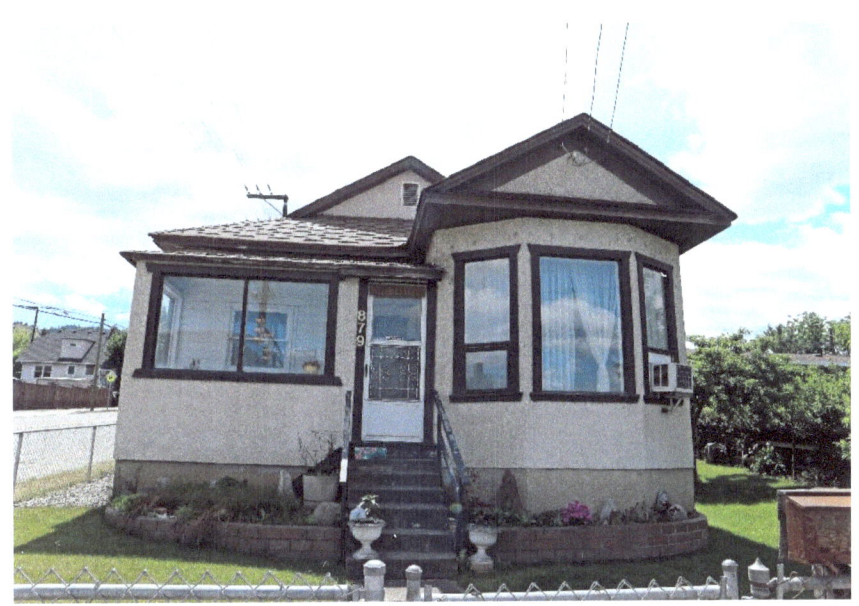

879 Columbia Street

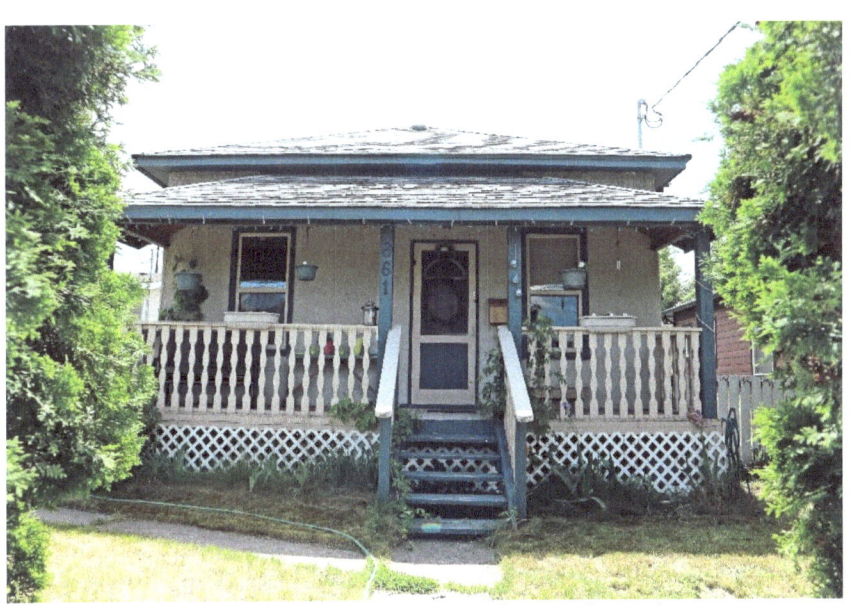

861 Columbia Street – hipped roof

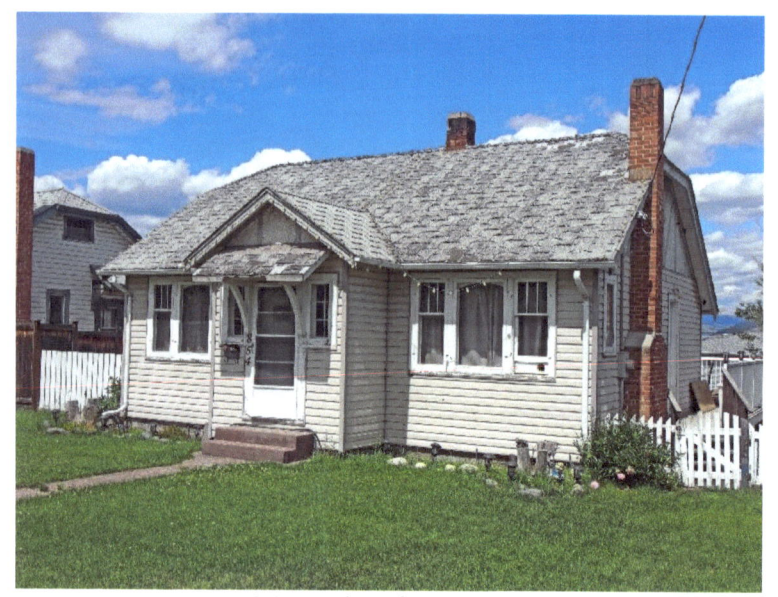
854 Columbia Street

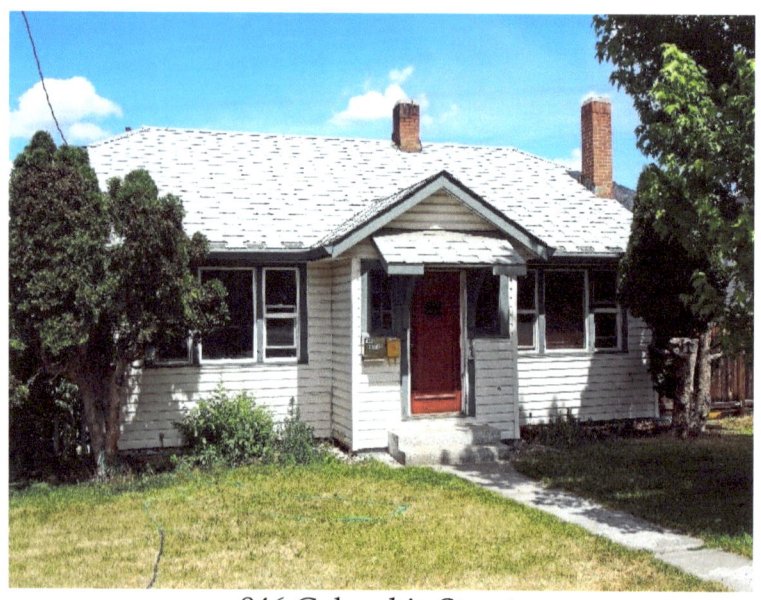
846 Columbia Street

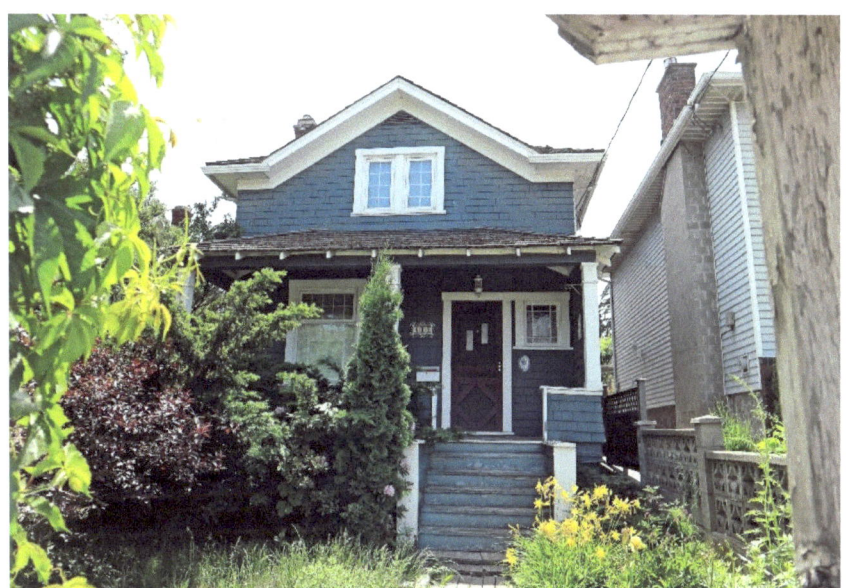

817 Columbia Street – Owen Norris House – Owen Norris settled in Kamloops in 1906. He was elected alderman in 1910 but he argued and clashed with the mayor. When Norris ran for mayor in 1911, he was soundly defeated. Norris left Kamloops the following year shortly after his new house on Columbia street was built, in 1912. Norris died a few short years later in Vancouver, in 1918.

This house could be a pre-fabricated house. Variations in the roof line and an 'eyebrow' window in the top peak soften the details of what is a Georgian Revival/Vernacular style house. Exposed rafter ends, details on the columns and the multipaned windows point to both the Queen Anne Revival and Craftsman styles.

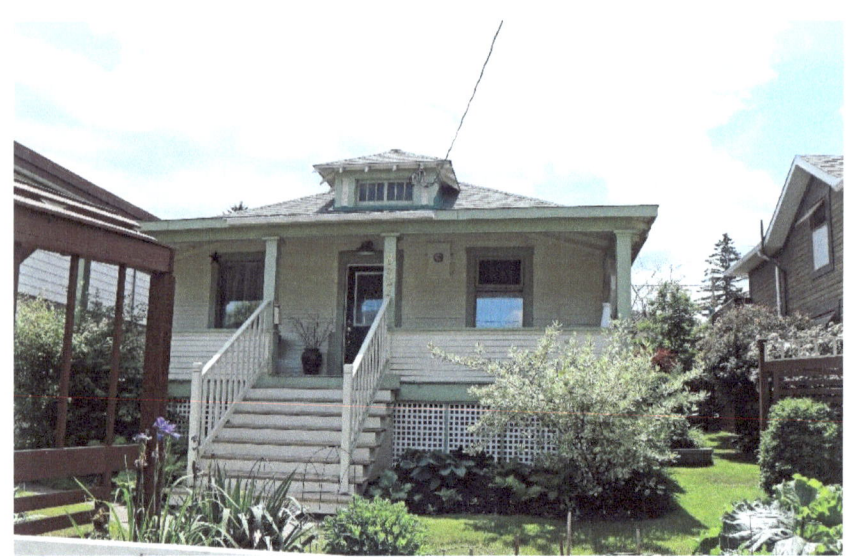

837 Columbia Street - dormer

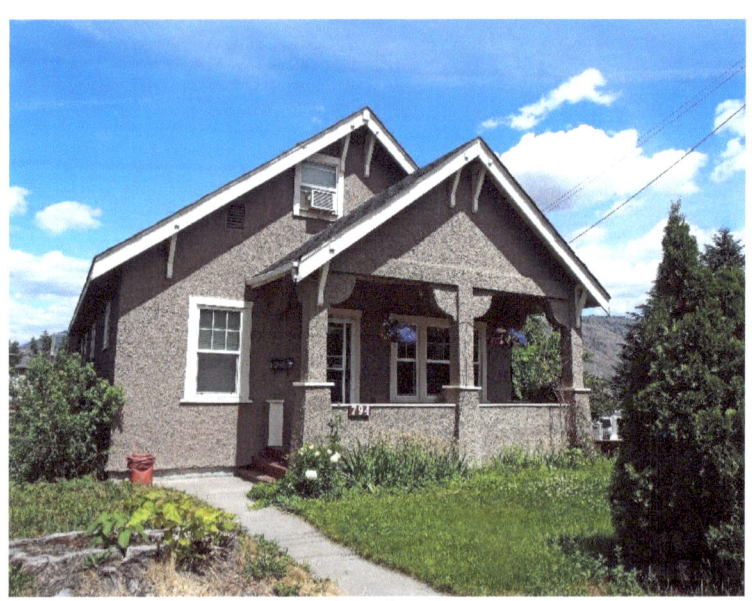

794 Columbia Street

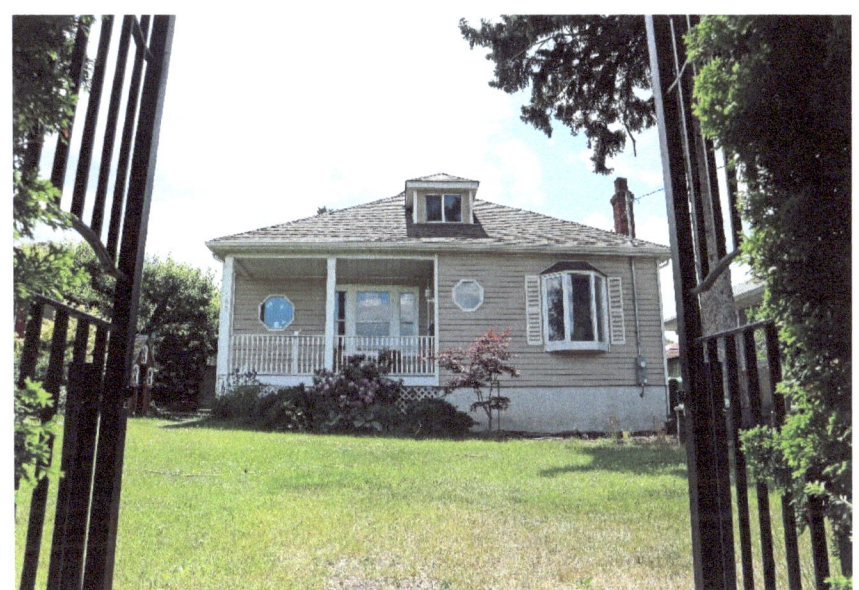

783 Columbia Street

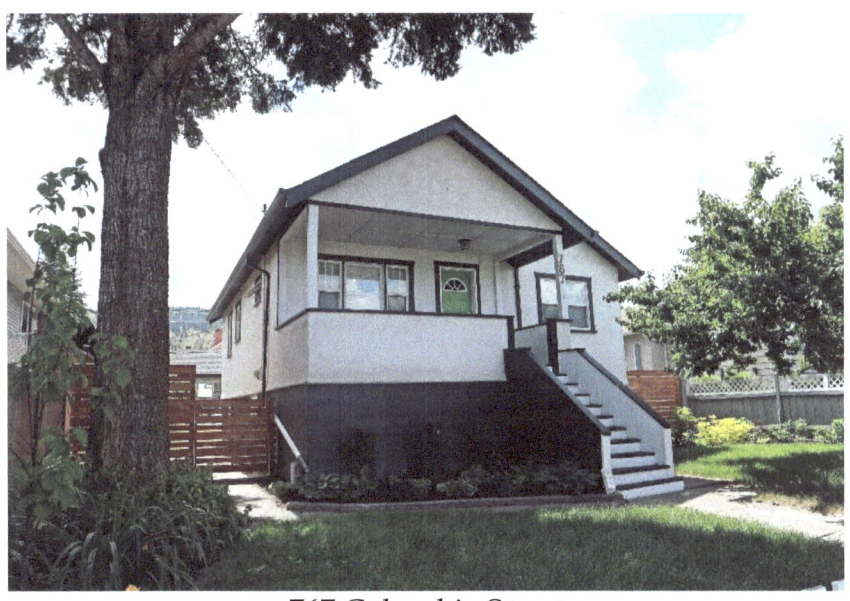

767 Columbia Street

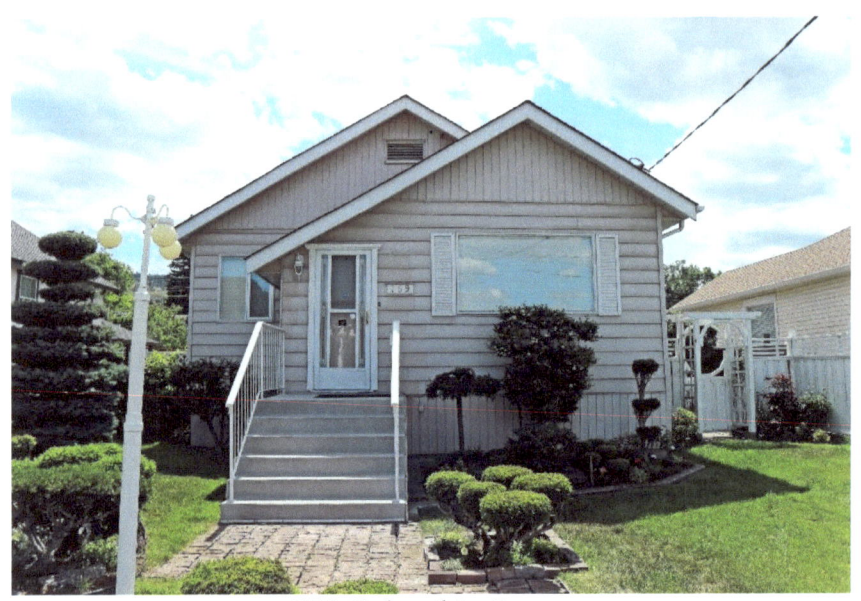

759 Columbia Street

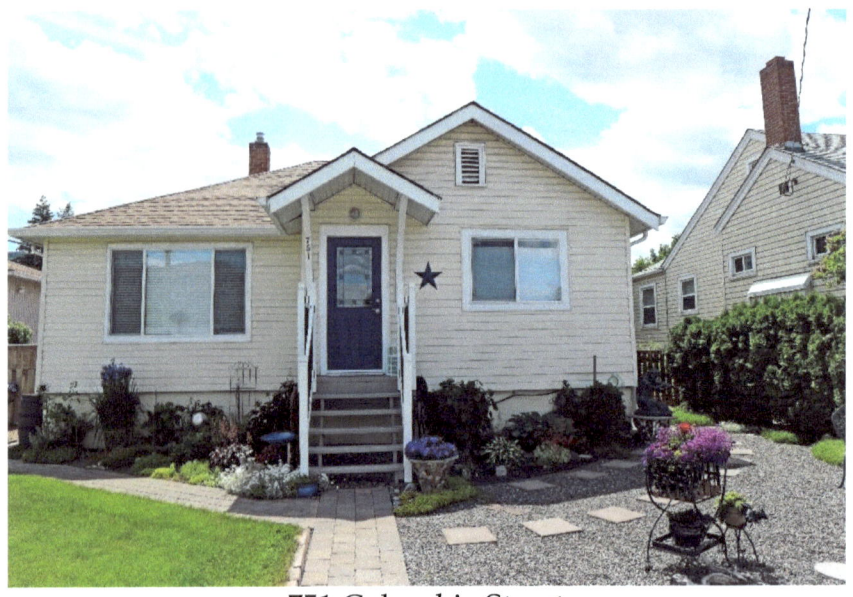

751 Columbia Street

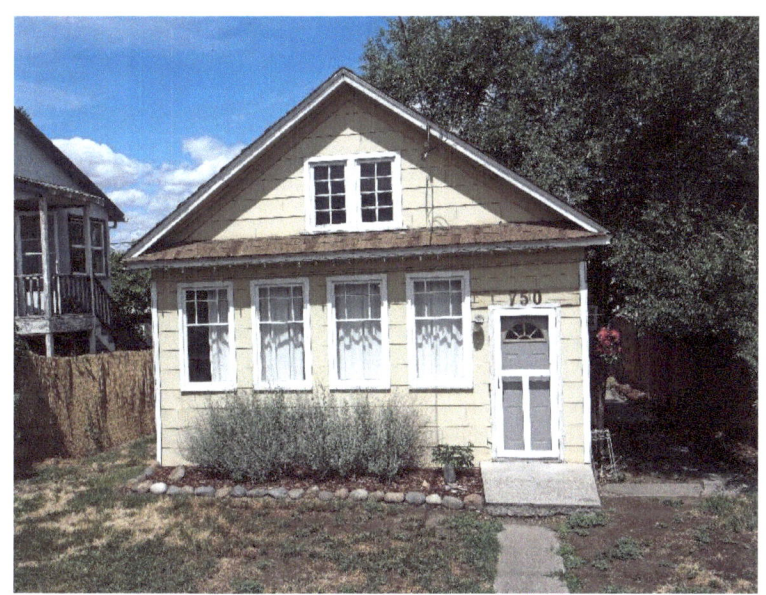
750 Columbia Street

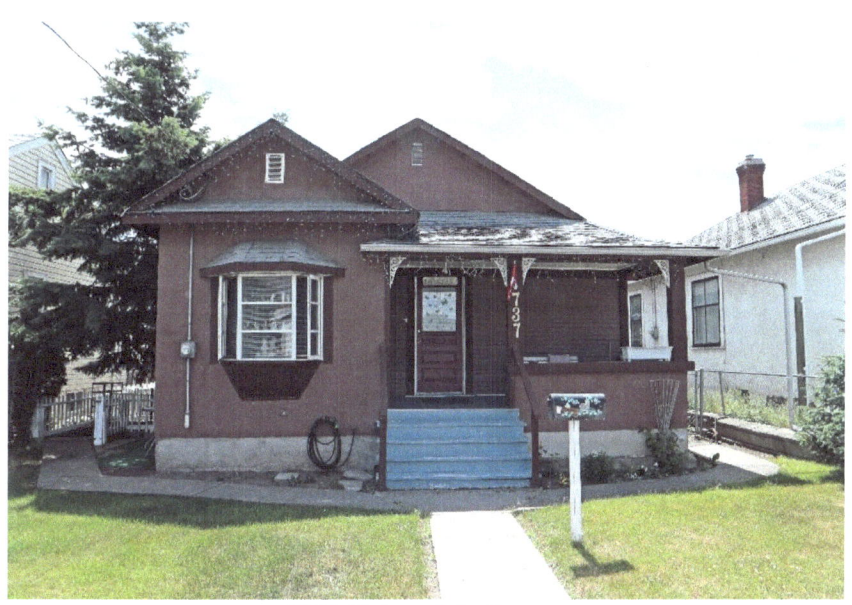
737 Columbia Street

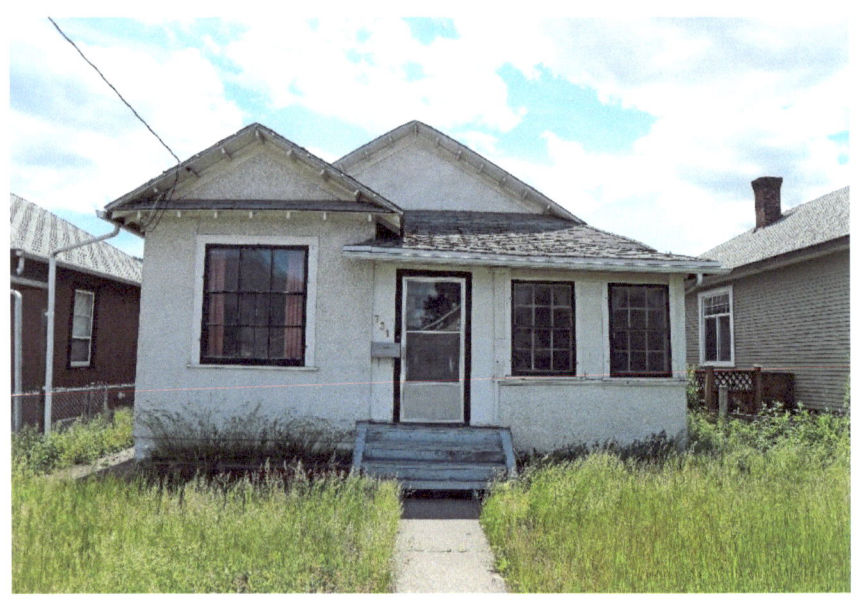

731 Columbia Street

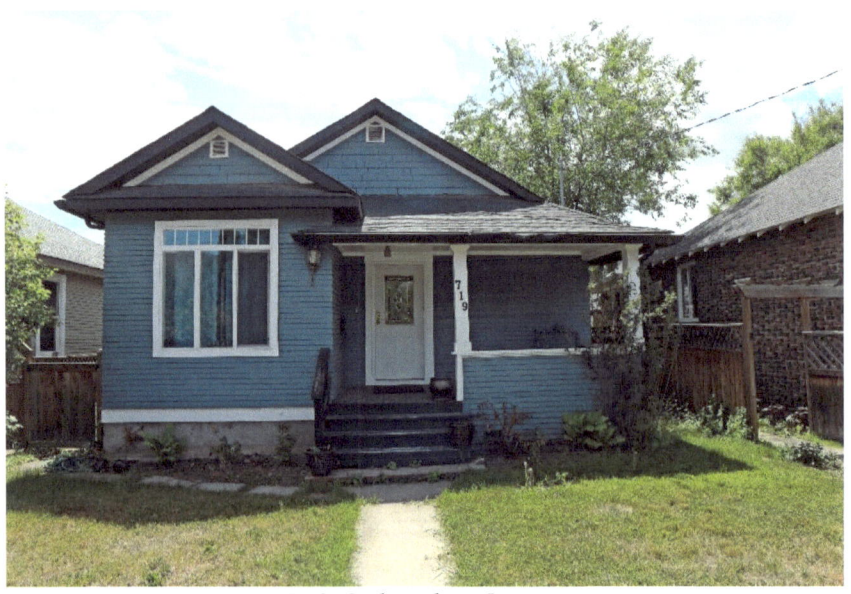

719 Columbia Street

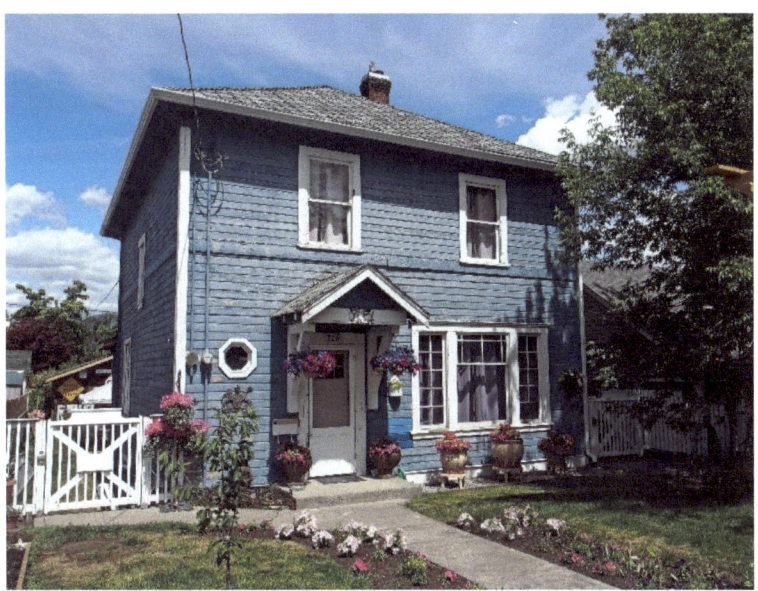

716 Columbia Street - Hargraves House - This house was built by C.H. Shutt in 1912 and became the family home of William and Margaret Hargraves in 1916. Margaret was an early Kamloops pioneer who arrived in 1878 while William came to the city in 1892. He had two previous marriages before he married Margaret Currie, a widow, in 1913.

William Hargraves was a very adaptable businessman. Starting with a blacksmith and bicycle repair shop he moved into owning a hardware store, the Isis movie theatre and then a Ford dealership. He was also an alderman during the 1907 - 1910 period but found politics too frustrating and preferred business ventures. He was a well-known local humorist who dressed up as John Bull, the iconic representation of England, for parades and sang comic songs at his theatre when the film broke.

The architectural style of this house is known as a Classic box structure that was popular in Kamloops at the beginning of the twentieth century. Original exterior features include multi-pane windows and clapboard siding.

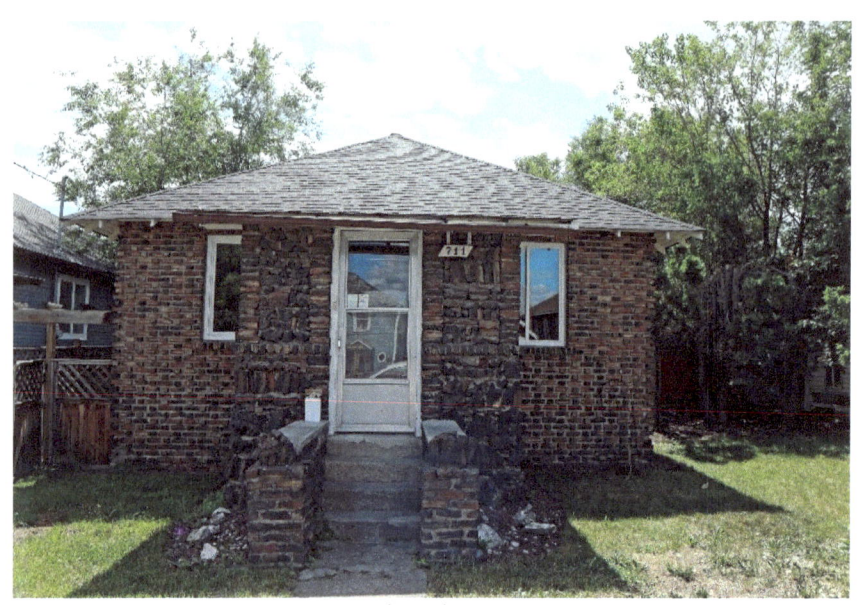
711 Columbia Street

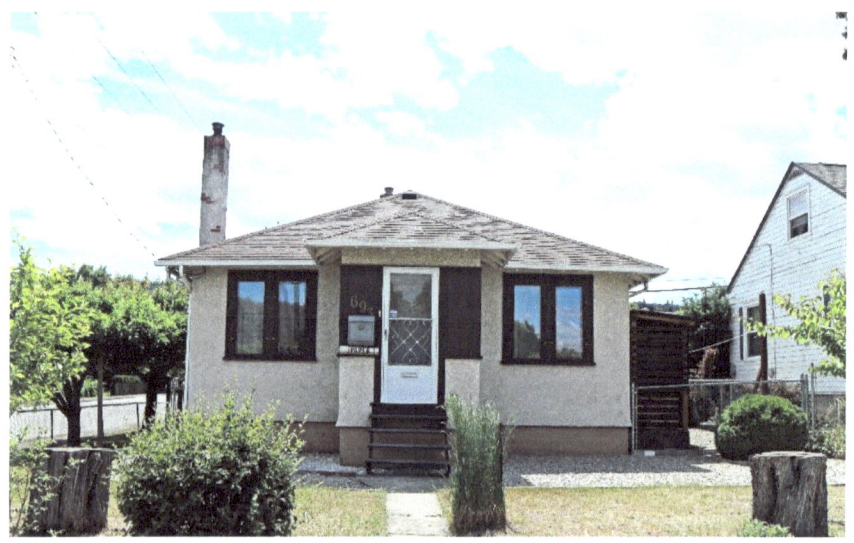
693 Columbia Street

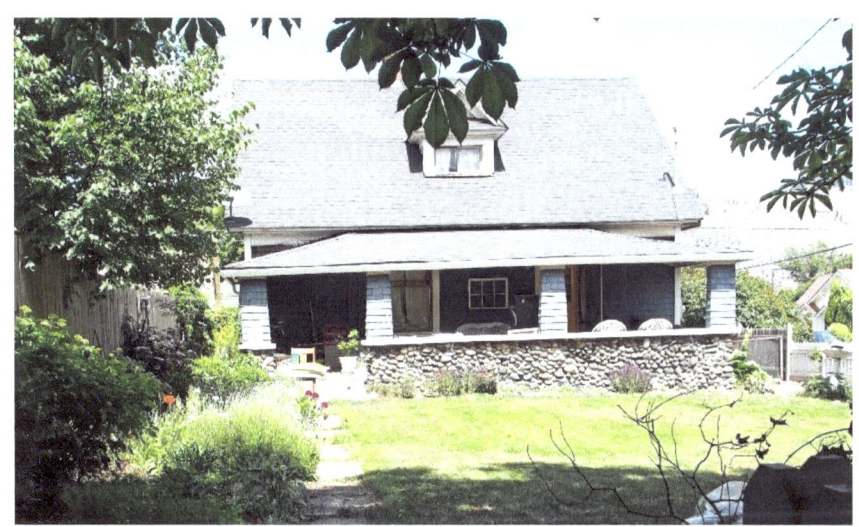

690 Columbia Street

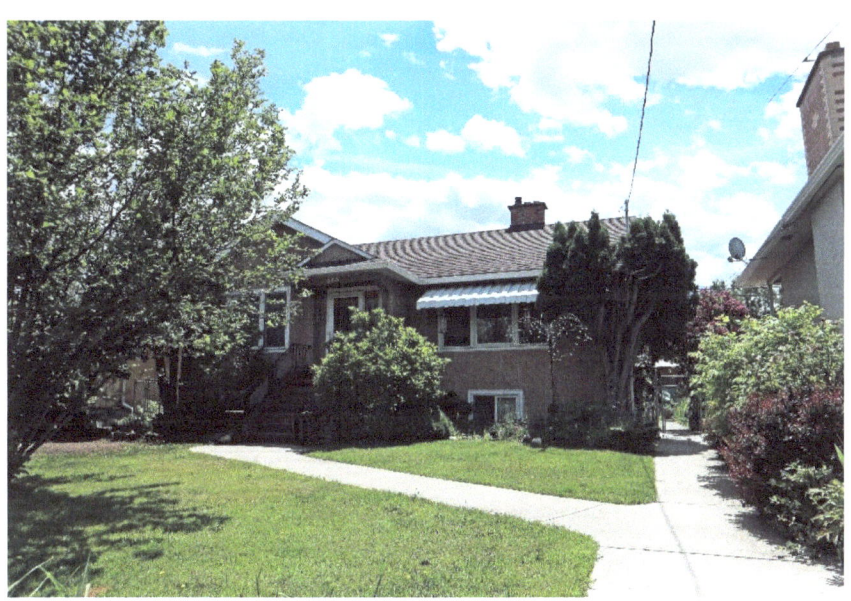

665 Columbia Street

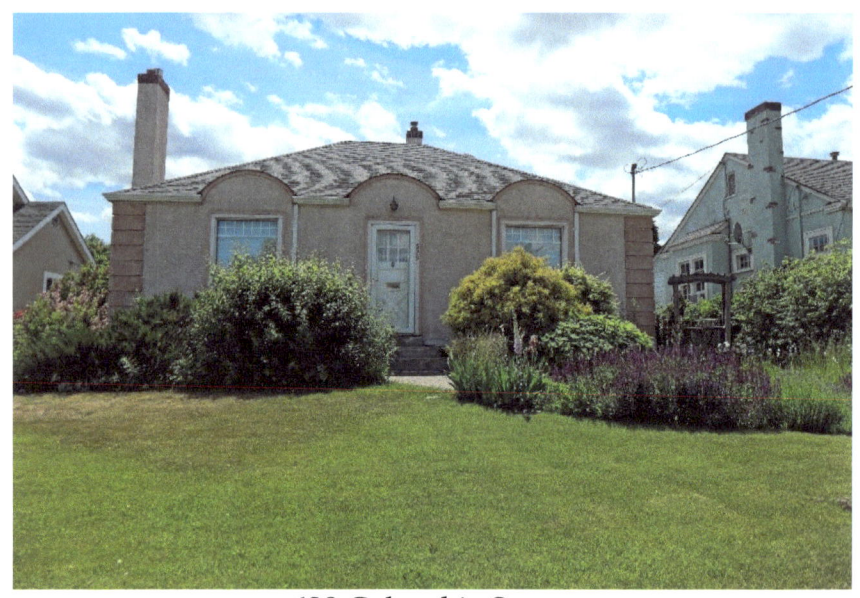

629 Columbia Street

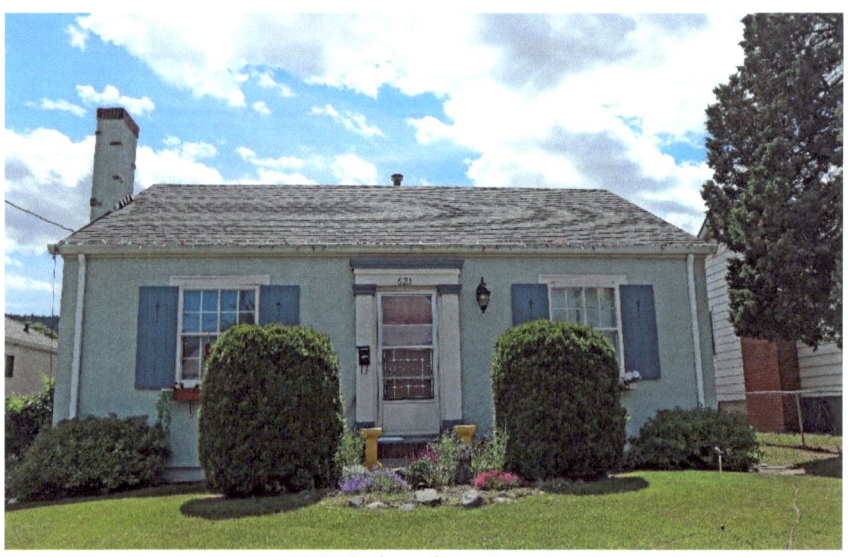

621 Columbia Street

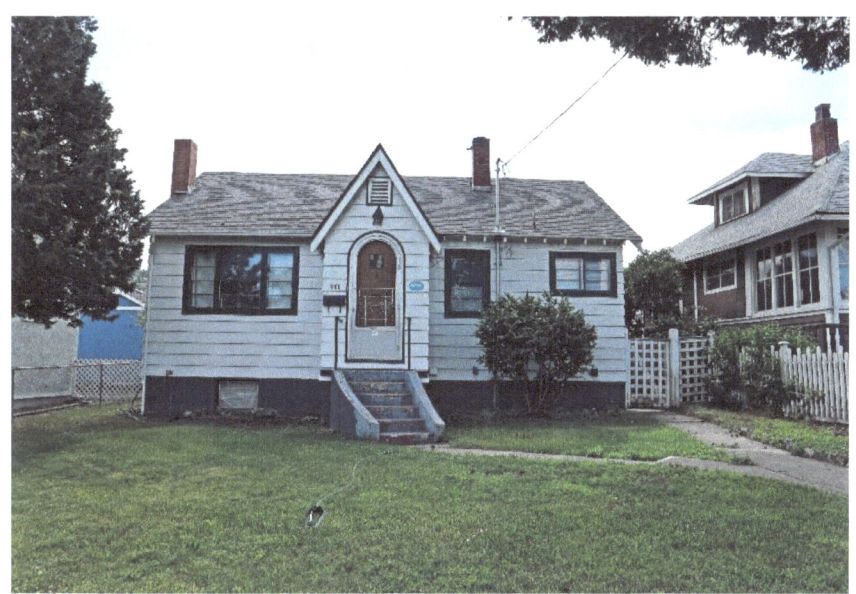

611 Columbia Street

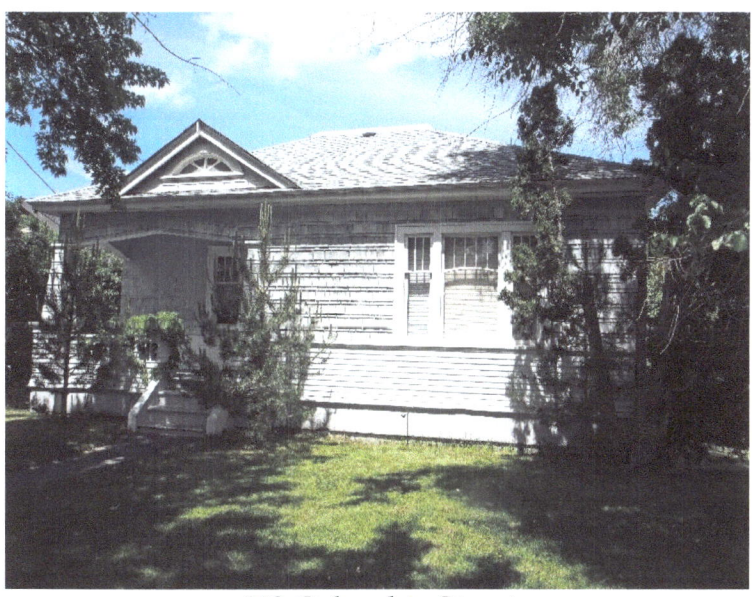

612 Columbia Street

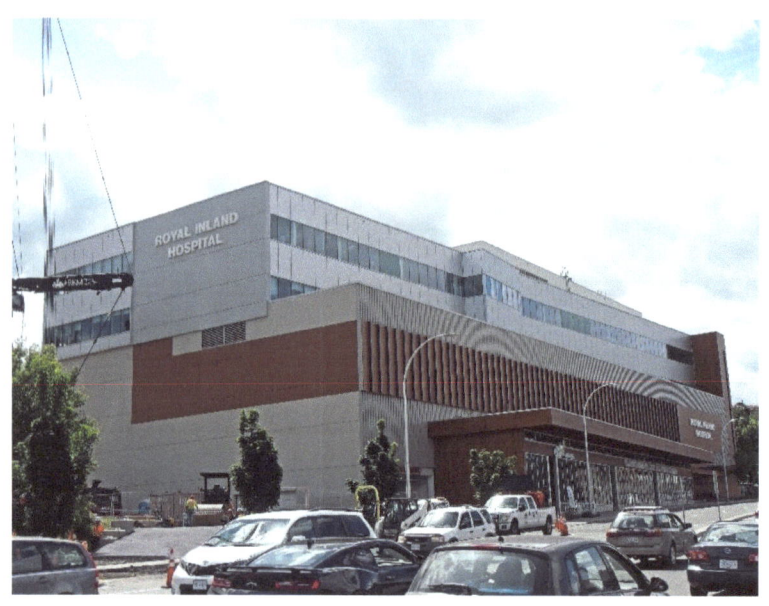

Columbia Street – Royal Inland Hospital

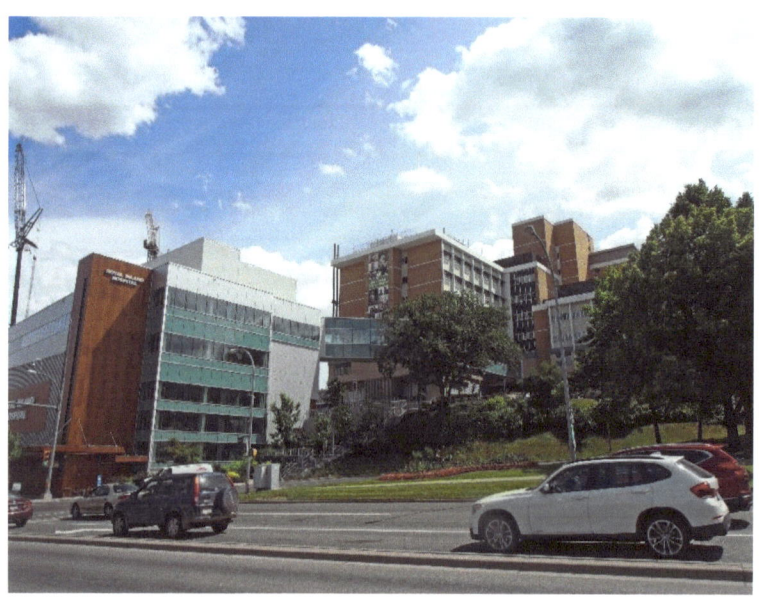

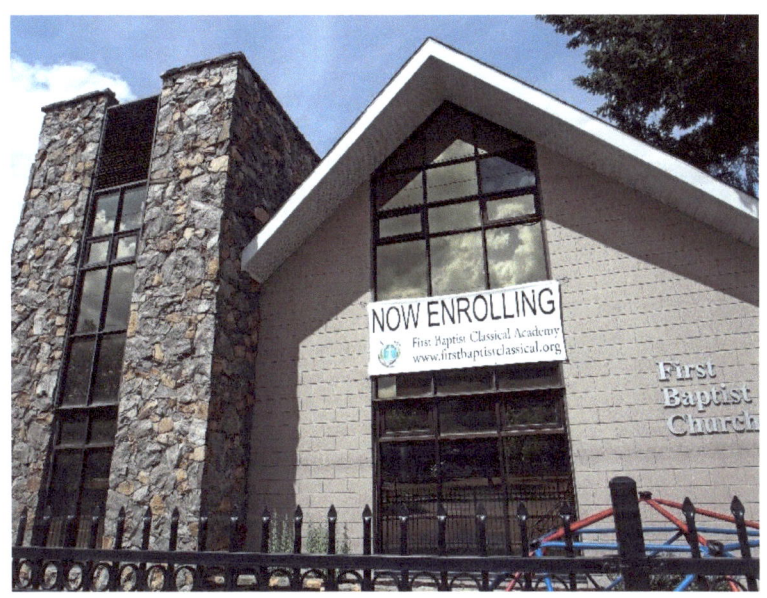

454 Columbia Street – First Baptist Church

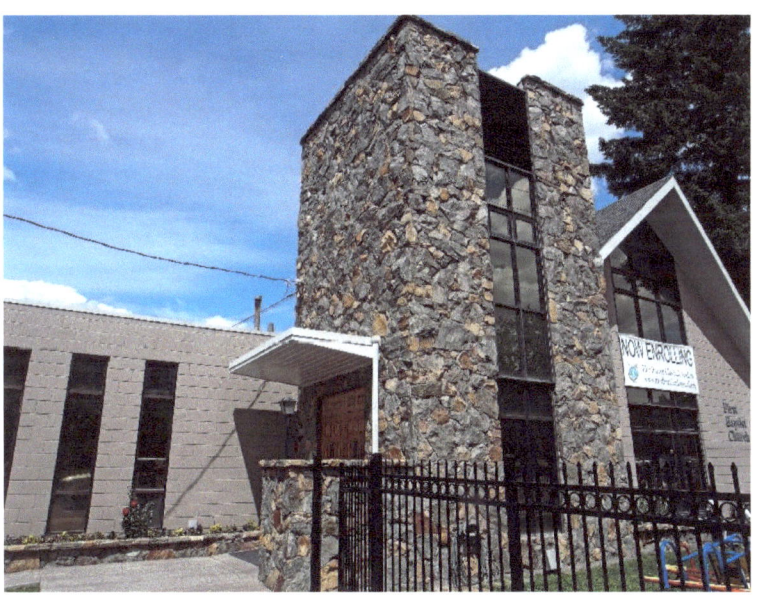

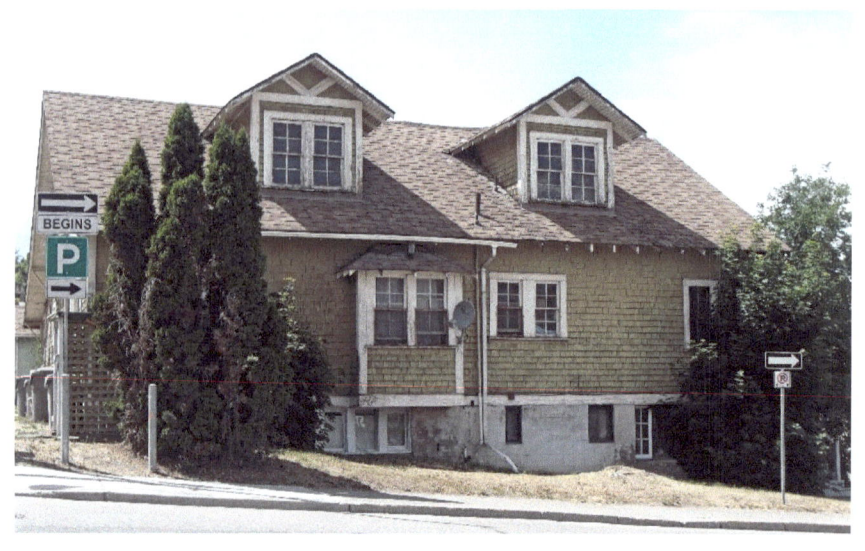

290 Columbia Street

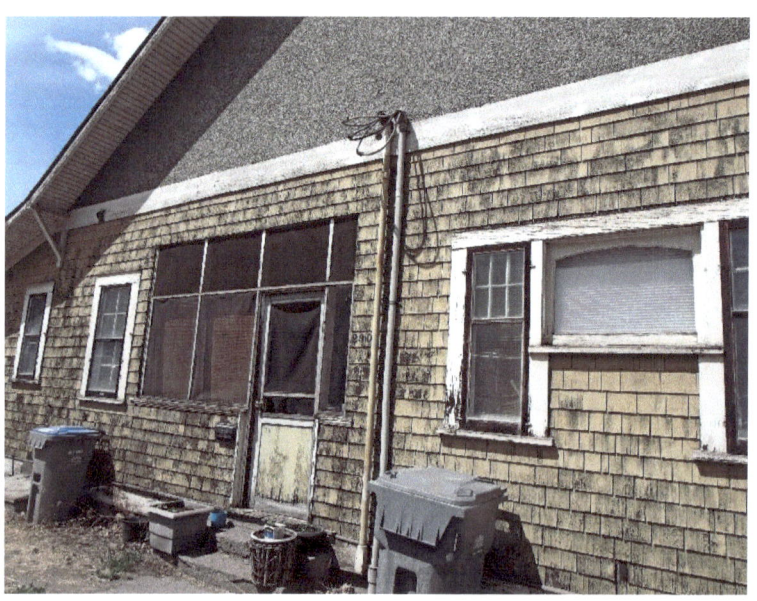

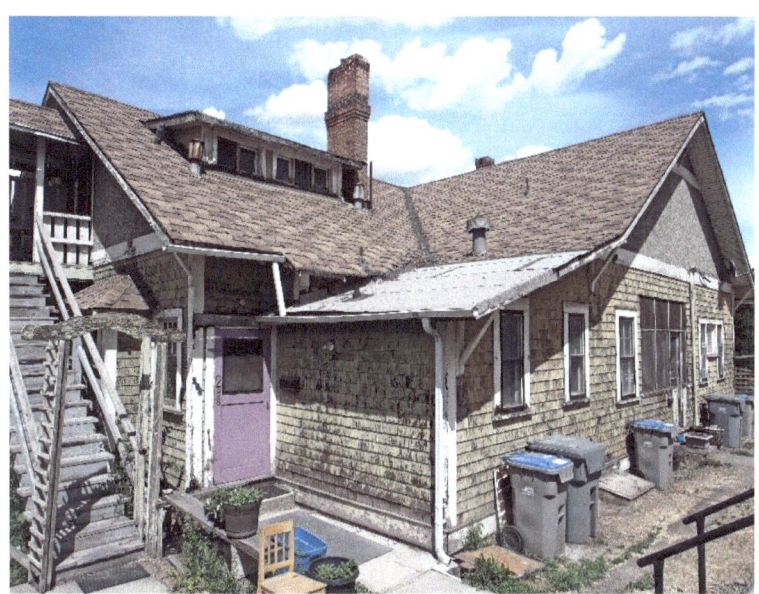

288-290 Columbia Street

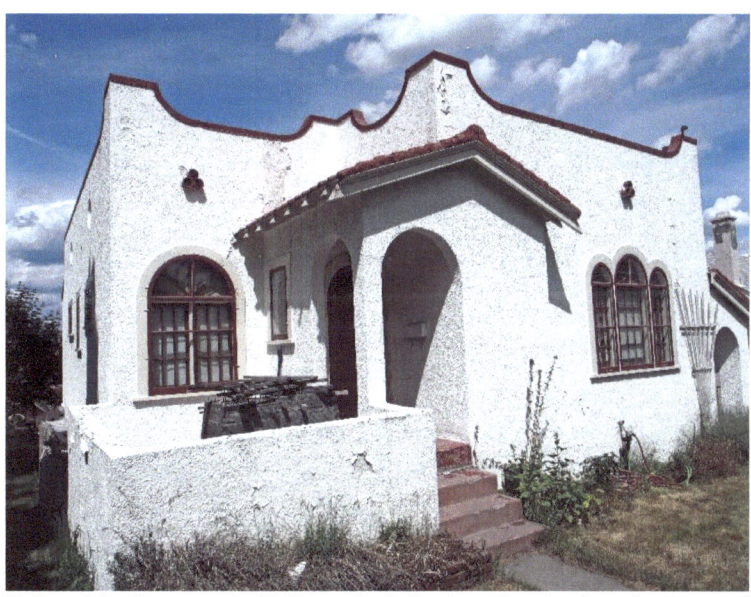

228 Columbia Street - A California Mission Revival style house built in 1931 using plans that the original owners brought from California. Exterior features include the flat roof with ornate parapet and windows with rounded arch construction.

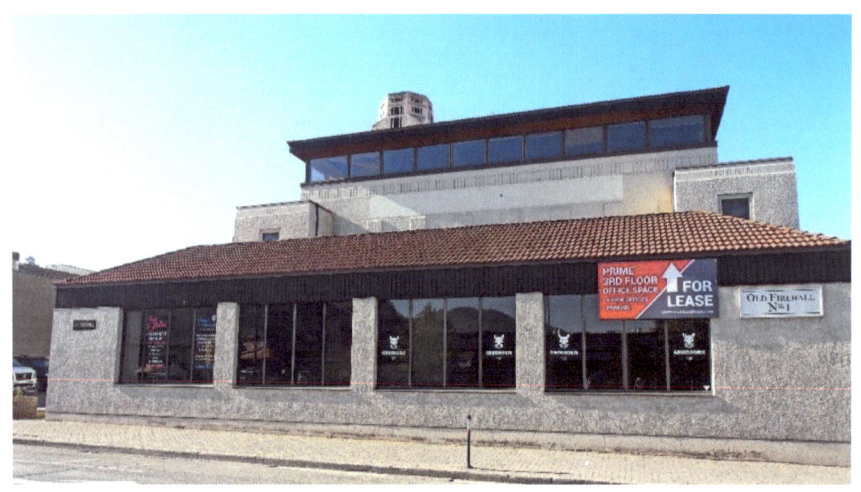

411 Lansdowne Street

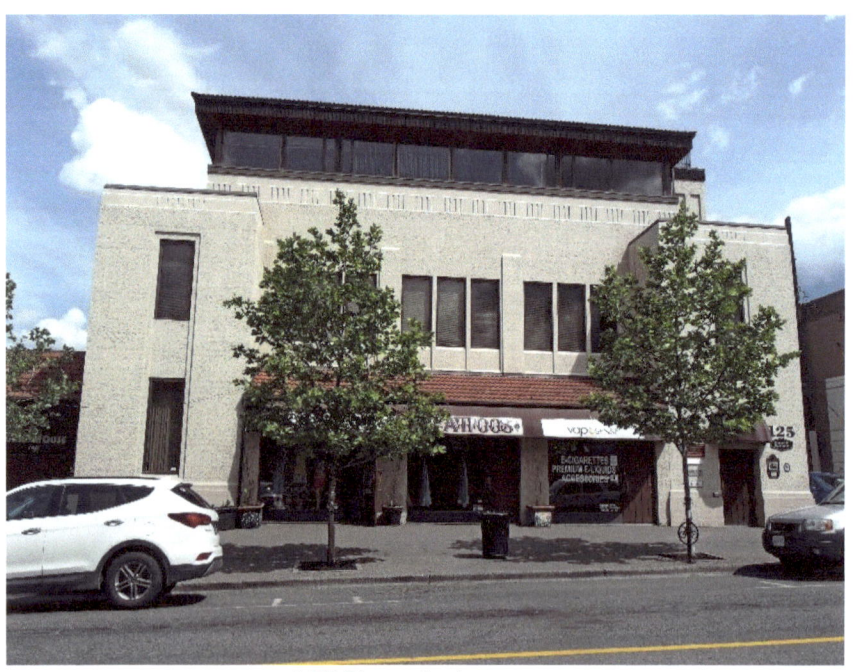

125 Fourth Avenue

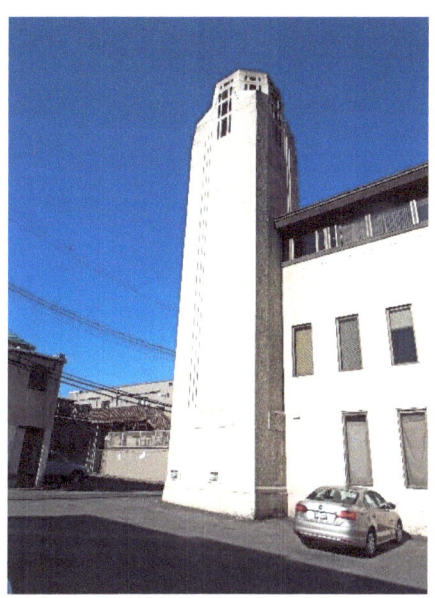

125 Fourth Avenue – Kamloops Firehall #1 (Spanish architecture style) was built in 1935 to replace Kamloops' first wood frame station on Victoria Street. The new station accommodated a larger fleet of fire trucks and a corps of volunteer and staff firefighters. There was an alarm system in the fire tower to call the volunteers to a fire.

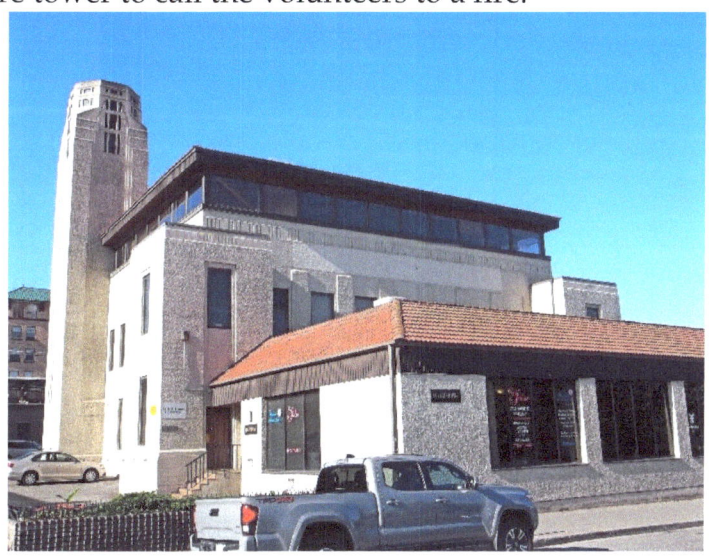

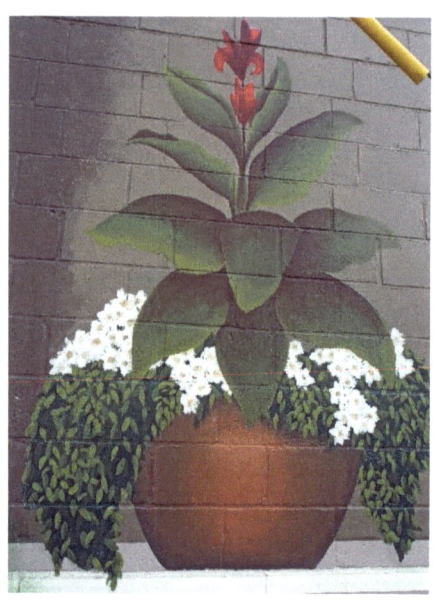

Hampton Art Gallery pictures on wall

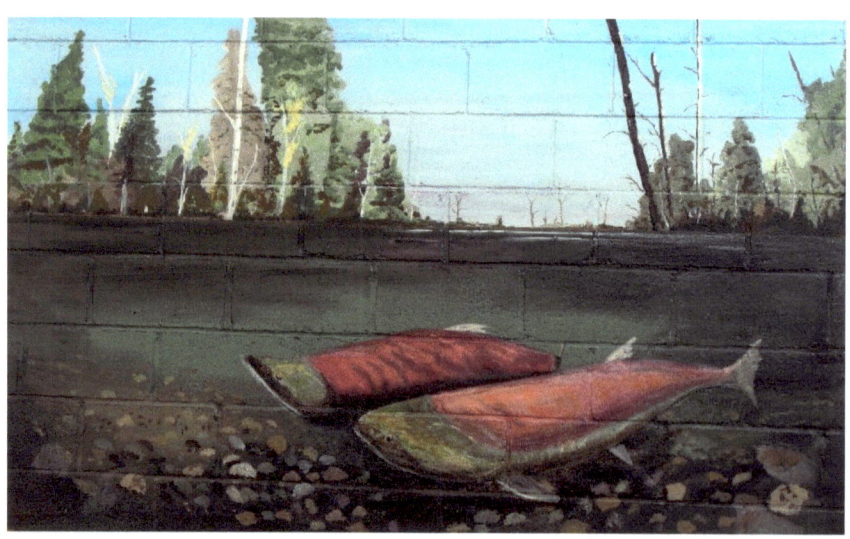

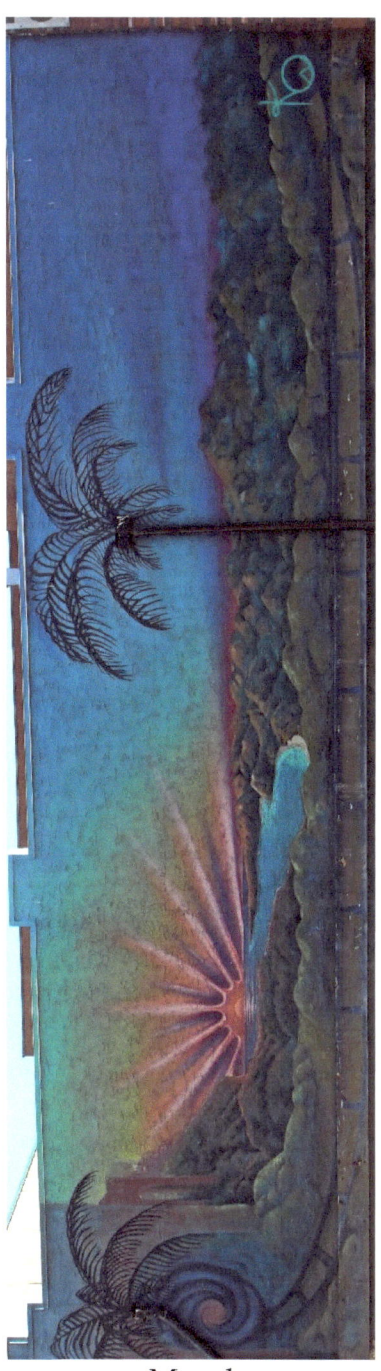

Mural

Series Name: Cruising Ontario, Saving Our History One Photo at a Time in colour photos

Books Available in Alphabetical Order:
Aberfoyle, Acton, Ajax, Alton, Amherstburg, Ancaster, Arthur, Auburn, Aylmer, Ayr, Beaver Valley, Belfountain, Belgrave, Belleville, Bloomingdale, Blyth, Brantford, Brockville, Burford, Burgessville, Burlington, Caledon, Caledonia, Cambridge, Carlow, Cayuga, Chatsworth, Cheltenham, Clifford, Colborne, Collingwood, Conestogo, Delhi, Dorchester to Aylmer, Drayton, Drumbo, Dundas, Dunlop, Dunnville, Eden Mills, Elmira, Elora, Embro, Erin, Essex, Fergus, Fort Erie, Georgetown, Goderich, Grimsby, Guelph, Hagersville, Haldimand County, Hamilton, Hanover, Harriston, Hespeler, Ingersoll, Inglewood, Innerkip, Jarvis, Kingston, Kingsville, Kitchener, Lake Superior, Lincoln, Linwood, Listowel, London, Lucknow, Merrickville, Mono, Mount Brydges, Mount Forest, Mount Pleasant, Neustadt, New Hamburg, Newboro, Newport, Niagara-on-the-Lake, Niagara Falls, North Bay, Norwich, Oakville, Onondaga, Orangeville, Orillia, Oshawa, Otterville, Owen Sound, Palmerston, Paris, Parry Sound, Pelham, Perth, Peterborough, Petrolia, Pickering, Port Colborne, Port Elgin, Port Hope, Port Perry, Portland, Preston, Rockwood, Sarnia, Sault Ste. Marie, Seaforth, Sheffield, Shelburne, Simcoe, Smiths Falls, Smithville, Southampton, Southwest Oxford, St. Catharines, St. George, St. Jacobs, St. Marys, St. Thomas, Stoney Creek, Stouffville, Stratford, Strathroy, Sudbury, Tavistock, Terra Cotta, Thamesford, Thunder Bay, Tillsonburg, Toronto, Uxbridge, Waterdown, Waterford, Waterloo, Welland, Wellesley, West Flamborough, Westport, Whitby, Windsor, Wingham, Woodstock, York, Zorra

Book 238-239: Ingersoll
Book 240: Zorra Township
Book 241: Southwest Oxford
Book 242: Otterville, Burgessville
Book 243: Norwich
Book 244: Woodstock Book 4

Other Books by Barbara Raue

Coins of Gold
Arrows, Indians and Love
The Life and Times of Barbara
The Cromwell Family Book
Laura Secord Discovered
Daddy Where Are You?

Montana Series
Book 1: Montana Dream
Book 2: Life on the Montana Frontier
Book 3: Montana to Boston and Back
Book 4: Montana Sons Go to War
Book 5: Montana Sons Return from War

Book 1: Rite of Passage
Book 2: Rite of Marriage

© 2019 by Barbara Raue - All the photos in this book have been taken with my cameras. I own the rights to them.

www.ingramcontent.com/pod-product-compliance
Lightning Source LLC
Chambersburg PA
CBHW040232220526
45473CB00001B/207